THE
LITTLE
BOOK
OF THE
ISLE OF
WIGHT

JAN TOMS

WITH ILLUSTRATIONS BY CATHERINE COX

First published 2011
Reprinted 2012

The History Press
The Mill, Brimscombe Port
Stroud, Gloucestershire, GL5 2QG
www.thehistorypress.co.uk

British Library Cataloguing in Publication Data.
A catalogue record for this book is available from the British Library.

ISBN 978 0 7524 5817 5

Typesetting and origination by
The History Press
Printed in Great Britain by TJ International Ltd, Padstow, Cornwall

CONTENTS

INTRODUCTION

There are two things that everyone knows about the Isle of Wight – Queen Victoria lived here and King Charles I was imprisoned in Carisbrooke Castle. Contrary to other assertions, the Island is not a tax haven, the natives don't speak French and visitors don't need a passport – although the Island MP Steve Ross once had his application refused by the passport office who claimed that the Isle of Wight was in the West Indies.

Things changed forever when Queen Victoria decided to buy 'dear, modest, unpretentious Osborne' set in a mere 1,727 acres of land – hardly room to swing a cat. She died there peacefully, although according to a teacher escorting children on a school trip, Her Majesty was shot in the drawing room.

King Charles indeed spent a year regretting his rash decision to pop over, being taken into 'protective custody' by the reluctant governor. Charles then spent a frenzied time sending coded letters and trying to climb out of windows. On leaving he probably wished that he had stayed, having a one-way ticket to the scaffold.

The Island has a wonderful coastline, spectacular scenery – and three prisons. From Parkhurst boys as young as eight were once transported to America and Australia and women prisoners rioted, taking off their clothes so that only married male officers armed with a blanket and a hose were brave enough to subdue them. In the twentieth century the Island played host to the Kray twins and the Yorkshire Ripper.

According to the Royal Medical and Chirurgical Society, the Island was an ideal place for 'weakly scrofulous children.' Queen Victoria's physician, Dr James Clark, went further, confirming that 'the several peculiarities of the climate…render it a highly favourable residence for invalids throughout the year.' If that failed, then Mr Greenham of Shanklin offered a nice line in invalid whiskey for 3/6d a bottle.

Edward Elgar spent his honeymoon in Ventnor while Jimi Hendrix gave his last performance on Afton Down. Lord Tennyson tried to hide away from his fans in Freshwater, referring to them as 'cockneys'. The summer season caused him to flee to the mainland.

General James Wolfe and Sir John Moore both spent their last nights in Newport before dashing off to find death and glory at Quebec and Corunna.

Calbourne Mill offers a home to a mammoth 19ft 2in gun weighing 38 tons that was formerly installed at Cliff End Fort. Its purpose was to guard the narrow opening between the Island and the Needles Channel but when it was tested in 1878, the resulting explosion caused so much damage to the fort that part of it had to be rebuilt. It was never fired again.

At the beginning of August 1914, Kaiser Wilhelm's yacht arrived in readiness for Cowes Week when, on 4 August, England declared war on Germany. The yacht made an ignominious retreat. At the same time, Prince Heinrich of Prussia – the Kaiser's brother – was taking the waters at the Spa Hotel at Shanklin. He quickly left in a taxi driven by Mr Sid Hackett.

Jan Toms, 2011

1

A BIT OF ISLAND HISTORY

WATCH OUT!

According to William Camden, the seventeenth-century historian, the Island 'is not so well fortified by its rocks and castles as by its inhabitants who are naturally warlike and courageous.' On the plus side, General Jack Seely, a rich mine owner whose family settled in the nineteenth century, reported that true islanders 'despised strangers but in an emergency, would risk life and limb to help them.'

Who were these 'Islanders'?

By the time William the Conqueror arrived, they were already a mixture of hunter-gathering, Roman, Anglo-Saxon, Jutish and Celtic Vikings with a dash of Nubian/Moorish blood thrown in. The Revd James White concluded that: 'the dark hair and brilliant eyes of the natives are derived from a Roman ancestry.'

The Island was probably the last place in Britain to be Christianised. J. Redding Ware was not impressed, writing that it 'was not a colossal achievement, for Caedwalla had put all the wretched islanders to the sword, with the exception of 300 families, who accepted the new faith as an exemption from death'. What would you have done?

The Domesday Book mentions eighty-four different places in the Isle of Wight, the names of the tenants reflecting their Saxon and Viking heritage. Looking for an unusual name for your son? How about: Alfsi, Alnoth, Ansketel, Bolla, Edric, Herbrand, Herpolf, Swarking, Thorald, Tovi, Wihtlac, Wulfsi. Technically they were now Norman but they carried on as before.

Here is a taste of 'Island speak': Wops – a wasp, Mallyshag – a pale green caterpillar of the large (cabbage) white butterfly, Emmet – an ant, Hoss stinger – a horse fly, Dumbledore – a large bumblebee, Galleybagger – a scarecrow, Knittles – a string used to tie up sacks –probably derived from the time when nettles were stripped and the stalks used as thread. Prate – the noise made by chickens, Chid – a young female sheep, also applied to young women, as in 'she's just a chid of a girl', Gimmer – an old ewe, probably one that was barren. The name was also used for widows, especially those housed in the workhouse, implying someone no longer of any use. A Gert Biggun – a great big one. Zummat – something, Wole – old, Bembridge weather – a rain shower when the sun is still shining, Scrouw – wet windy weather. Shrammed – chilled to the bone. A Luccomber – a squall coming around Dunnose point from the south. Nammet – a 'ploughman's lunch' taken by workmen into the fields along with ale to drink, currently applied to a coffee break – 'elevenses'. Nipper – from the seafaring habit of getting lads to nip up the rigging on ships; often applied humorously from one older man to another in memory of their lost youth. The Screws – vivid description of joint pain, probably arthritis. Queer – having two distinct meanings, neither relating to being strange or to sexual orientation. To *feel* queer is to feel unwell, while to *be* queer means to be annoyed about something.

A native Islander is an Isle of Wight Calf, the derivation too old to trace. They are also called Caulkheads, allegedly because of the Island preoccupation with the sea and caulking boats to make them waterproof. Some people call them Corkheads, implying that they are so empty headed that they float.

Island pronunciations of towns and villages: Isle of Wight – Oil o'Woight, Newport – Neppert, Ryde – Roide, Shorwell – Shorrel, Shalfleet – Shufflet, Swainston – Swanston, Whitwell – Whittle, Brighstone – Brighstone – It was known as Brixton but the Islanders won the day, Bowcombe – Buckham.

Some local surnames surviving from Domesday times: Ballard, Barrett, Brett, Buckett, Burt, Calloway, Caws, Cheverton, Dingley, Dore, Downer, Erlesman, Fallick, Harvey, Holbrooke, Jolliffe, Kent, Kingswell, Lacey, Lale, Mackett, Meulx (Mew), Rayner, Salter, Serle, Trickett, Tutton, Urry, Wavell, Woodnutt.

More local surnames surviving from at least Elizabethan times: Angell, Attrill, Barton, Baskett, Blow, Champion, Cheke, Colenutt, Cotton, Fleming, Frissell, Galpin, Gosden, Goter, Leigh, Merwood, Millmore,

Newland, Pragnell, Rudge, Siggins, Sheath, Stallard, Trenchard, Wade, Westmore, Woodford – spellings were at best idiosyncratic.

Carving the Island up. The Island was once divided into two districts, the East and West Medine, the river Medina being the boundary.

The East Medine consisted of Brading, Wootton, Yaverland, Whippingham, Shanklin, Arreton, Bonchurch, St Helens, St Lawrence, Newchurch, Whitwell, Binstead and Niton.

West Medine was made up of Northwood, Brixton (Brighstone), Carisbrooke, Calbourne, St Nicholas, Mottistone, Gatcombe, Brook, Chale, Shalfleet, Kingston, Thorley, Shorwell, Yarmouth, Freshwater and Newport.

SOME FACTS ABOUT THE ISLAND'S TOWNS AND VILLAGES

Yarmouth is the smallest town in the United Kingdom with a population of about 1,000, while the neighbouring village of Freshwater has a population five times as large.

Bembridge claims to be the biggest village in the UK, although its population is smaller than Freshwater. The Romans exported Bembridge limestone to the mainland to build Fishbourne Palace near Chichester.

The hamlet of Limerstone was the site of an ancient manor and chapel employing three priests. The heiress, Isabella, who married Sir Roger de Tichborne, was famed for her good works.

Niton was once known as Niton Regis, being part of the manor of King Edward the Confessor.

Rookley was in the eighteenth and nineteenth century the distribution point for smuggled goods. It is estimated that in 1840 alone, 100,000 casks of spirits were brought ashore around the coast.

Praise in 1794 that Newport was a 'well built, handsome town, the shops are numerous and, as superbly stocked as they are in most of the English cities.' Rather more snootily, the writer thought that:

'The little hamlet of Norton exhibits some rural cottages that have lately been erected, with more expense than taste.'

Borthwood is a corruption of Broadwood, for the type of trees long growing there. Island oaks furnished much of the navy, it taking upwards of 700 trees to build one warship.

In 1844, Samuel Landon, 'the biggest man in the world', was buried in the churchyard of the Holy Cross, Binstead.

Chillerton epitomises village life in Victorian times. The 1861 census reveals 191 inhabitants and only four were not born locally. Village occupations nearly all depended on agriculture. There were blacksmiths, shepherds, ploughboys, cowboys, carters, carpenters, with most listed simply as agricultural labourers. Sixty-five children attended the village school. There were two non-conformist chapels and a pub – the Foxhound, the landlord also working as a carpenter. The village now has few of those Victorian families' descendants, and even less of the occupations that once supported them.

Shanklin owed its early popularity to three factors – a sandy bay, the discovery of health-giving waters and the presence of the Chine. In 1903, a visitor enthused: 'What more beautiful spot in all the Island can you behold than Shanklin Chine? Artificial beauty? Oh no, the hand of the gardener or his spade never comes here: this is Nature, she plants and trims herself.'

He fell in love with the 'huge, magnificent chestnut tree' that overhung the Old Village – alas no more, and the 'beautiful swans disporting themselves' on the duck pond, also sadly absent although ducks are in abundance. Regrettably neither does one hear the 'loud tones of the town clock ring over the town every hour of the twenty-four'. Most public clocks have long since been silenced.

Following the discovery of Ventnor by the Victorians, John Betjeman observed that 'Little Osbornes' were built on every available piece of cliff, every ledge and cranny and each Little Osborne had its garden of palms, myrtles and hydrangeas and its glimpse of the sea.

According to the father-in-law of Samuel Wilbeforce (one of the three bishops after whom the pub at Brighstone is named), the village was 'notorious for villainy and loose living due to the influence of the barracks and smugglers.'

Time For a Cuppa?

The Edinburgh Wool Mill shop in Newport's High Street is the likely site of Smith's grocery shop. Here, Job Smith sold his brother-in-law John Horniman's first ever packaged tea.

Hard Cheese

The Island once had its own brand of cheese made with skimmed milk. It was so hard that it was known locally as Isle of Wight Rock. Having bought a consignment that he could not sell, a local grocer placed it outside his shop in the hope that locals would take it away. The following morning, two cheeses had gone. Leaving them out again, the next day he discovered that the stolen cheeses had been returned!

The Right to Vote

The Island is the biggest parliamentary constituency in the country. Between 1295 and 1584 however no one represented it in Parliament. Although they had a right to nominate someone, being an insular lot the Islanders preferred to avoid the expense.

When the first Queen Elizabeth's cousin, Sir George Carey, came to make the Island ready for Spanish invasion he negotiated that Yarmouth, Newport and Newtown should each send two men to Parliament, promptly nominating his brother as MP for Newport. At the time the Island population was under 9,000 and for nearly 300 years it continued to be represented by six men.

Island MPs have included the Duke of Marlborough and the Prime Ministers Canning, Melbourne, Palmerston and Wellington. It wasn't until 1885 that the Island was reduced to one MP.

Women over thirty were given the right to vote in 1918, when 17,535 Island girls swelled the electorate to 41,718. Twenty years later the local Liberals selected the first female candidate in Helen Simpson, an Australian novelist and wife of a Harley Street consultant. Tragically, she died early so any future advance to Parliament was halted.

Saving One's Bacon?

Before the 1949 General Election, the Labour Party held its conference at Shanklin Manor. About sixty members of the NEC arrived including Clement Attlee, Ernest Bevin, Aneurin Bevan, Sir Stafford Cripps, Dr Edith Summerskill and a young Harold Wilson. A crisis arose when the organisers ran out of glasses but was averted when the Conservative Club magnanimously supplied them.

Not so simple was the discovery that in these days of rationing, the organisers had overrun their bacon ration by 2lbs. They were prosecuted, thus ending an historic visit. The Labour Party 'Bigwigs' have not been back since.

Happy Retirement?

On 1 January 1909, David Lloyd George introduced old age pensions. Ranging between 1/- and 5/- (5p and 25p) they were available only to those whose income was less than 12/- (60p) a week. 1,300 Islanders qualified.

EDUCATION

Latin or Lager?

In 1855, Miss Lucy Strange of Shanklin advertised her services in running a boarding school and as a beer retailer.

Good Attendance?

Rookley School took the prize for 100 per cent attendance in 1906. This was achieved only at the last minute when one pupil physically carried his friend to school each day because he had a sprained ankle. He should have gone far, that boy!

Work

The gayest time in Newport was to be had at the Whitsuntide Fair and on three successive Saturdays at Michaelmas, when agricultural servants received their wages and were re-engaged for the following year.

In 1826, a new factory arrived in Newport. Coming from Nottingham, the home of lace-making, Mr W.H. Nunn and his family moved to the island where he began to produce expensive French, blond lace, in a honey colour woven in fine silk. In 1833, Mr Nunn took out a patent for an improved machine and at its height the factory employed some 200 people. This useful employment ended in 1870 on Mr Nunn's death, when the factory closed. His heiress, Mary, turned the premises into a rest home for the elderly. The building is currently a local government office. Mary and her father are buried at St Paul's Church, Barton, close to the factory site.

When wigs were in fashion, Newport was the Island centre for the manufactory of starch and hair powder, 'which consumes a great quantity of flour, the duty of which alone amounts to £3,000.'

Saving for the Future?
A branch of the Isle of Wight Trustees Savings bank opened at Calbourne in 1834

What's in a Name?
In his book *Egypt and the Isle of Wight*, Rendel Harris concludes that the Island was colonised by Egyptians, this based on place names that could be construed as having an Egyptian origin. The following words back up his theory: Chine – the Egyptian word for cut is 'tcha' and the chines are cuts into the cliff. Yar as in the river and Yarmouth – the Egyptian word 'yor' means river. Medina, as in the river, is in his opinion self-evident Medina being the sacred Arabic city.

The Egyptians made use of woad and that too can be deduced from the names Woodhouse and Wootton, deriving from woad house and woad ton.

As if that isn't proof enough, what about apse as in Apse Heath and also apes as in Apesdown that is reminiscent of the Egyptian sacred bull – this does sound rather like a lot of sacred bull.

X Marks the Spot!
During the English Civil War, fearing attack by the parliamentary forces, royalist Eustace Mann buried his treasure in the grounds of his estate at Osborne. When the threat had passed he went to retrieve it but could not locate the spot. As far as is known, it was never recovered. The area is still known as Money Coppice.

In the wall of the thatched church at Freshwater Bay is a stone bearing the date 1622. In fact, the church was built on land donated by Lord Tennyson's son Hallam in 1910. The dated stone came from a demolished farmhouse in Hooke Hill, where Robert Hooke, the inventor and scientist was born in 1635. His father was the local curate.

The building on the corner of Holyrood Street and Crocker Street at Newport was once the Sun Inn and extending above Reads Livery Stables were the Assembly Rooms, a ballroom where local society

dances took place. Here, young bloods in military uniform, wealthy farmers and young ladies guarded by chaperones cavorted all night. The club had a rule that all wagers and debts should be paid only in claret or Madeira. It lasted from 1760 to 1820.

Listed Buildings

The Island has nearly 2,000 listed buildings. Following English Heritage guidelines, they are divided into three sections – grades 1, II* and 2.

Grade 1, unsurprisingly, comprises the most important and there are twenty-six, of which twelve are churches. The churches are St George's, Arreton; St Mary's, Brading; St Mildred's, Whippingham; St Olave's, Gatcombe; All Saints, Godshill; All Saints, Newchurch; St Mary's, Carisbrooke; St Thomas's, Newport; St John the Baptist,

Northwood; St John the Baptist, Yaverland; Church of St Michael the Archangel, Shalfleet and St Peter's in Shorwell.

The secular buildings are Osborne House at East Cowes, Appuldurcombe House at Wroxall, Carisbrooke Castle and Yarmouth Castle, all administered by English Heritage while the windmill at Bembridge is under the guardianship of the National Trust.

Of the others, the Roman Villa at Brading and the Roman Villa at Newport are open to the public.

Norris Castle in East Cowes, the Bailiff's House at Norris Castle Farm, Farringford House at Freshwater, Golden Hill Fort at Freshwater, the Roman Villa at St Mary's Vicarage Carisbrooke, Yaverland Manor at Sandown and Wolverton Manor at Shorwell are all privately owned.

There are fifty-six grade II* buildings, most on a par with the list above. They include Arreton Manor, Haseley Manor, Nunwell House, Northwood House, Newport Grammar School, God's Providence House at Newport (a restaurant), the George Inn at Newport and the Bugle in Yarmouth.

Also listed are tombstones, a mounting block (Hasely Manor), a telephone kiosk (Bembridge High Street), a drinking fountain (Bembridge), a hammerhead crane (Cowes), bridges at Beacon Alley Godshill and Newtown Creek, an animal pound at Brading, seven water hydrants at Whitwell and the railway station at Shanklin.

THE WORKHOUSE

An all-Island Workhouse opened in about 1800 – the first in the country. It was erected where St Mary's Hospital now stands and until recently the original red-brick building was used as a geriatric ward. Men were separated from women, husbands from wives and children from parents.

Work involved knitting, labouring in the fields at harvest time, filling potholes in the roads and that old task, oakum picking – unravelling frayed, tarred rope so that the threads could be re-used. Diet included a preponderance of bread and potatoes with a few pieces of meat and veg thrown in.

Clothes were changed weekly and bed linen monthly. For the first few years there were not enough beds to go round and inmates had to share.

Ostracised

The worst to suffer were unmarried mothers, who were separately housed and had their names recorded in a Black Book. They wore coarse yellow gowns to distinguish them from the 'respectable' women.

In 1881, the workhouse contained 377 inmates ranging in age from three months to ninety-two years. Of these, 110 were children.

Idiot, Imbecile or Lunatic?

These three categories were routinely listed in the admittance book although the differences are uncertain. The dictionary definition for both idiot and imbecile is a person of subnormal intelligence. An idiot is defined as having a mental age of less than three while an imbecile's mental abilities were stated to be 'well below par'. Lunatic was simply described as 'insane'. In 1881 there were forty such persons. Until the Island's mental asylum opened at Whitecroft in 1896, lunatics were shipped across the water to Laverstock in Wiltshire.

Others marked out for distinction were the blind, the deaf and the dumb. Behind the facts were real people and one must wonder what became of them.

IDIOT   IMBECILE   LUNATIC

Apprenticeships

Where possible, the young were apprenticed. The greatest number went into 'husbandry', in other words were lined up for farm work. The terms of the agreement between master and workhouse varied from three to seven years. Girls were invariably trained as domestic servants.

Those taking on an apprentice followed a variety of trades. There was surprising number of 'hairdressers' that might have involved dressing the then fashionable wigs and powdered hair. Others included a pipe maker, mangler, builder, mercer, maltster, hatter, baker, grocer and confectioner, several vicars, a surgeon, an attorney, Mr Nunn, who ran the lace factory at Newport, and Mr Pittis, the local auctioneer, both took on workhouse children.

Old and Peculiar Street and Place Names

Yarmouth: Adder Street, Snake Street, Saddler's Lane, Goldsmith Street and Bowling Alley.

Newport: Deadman's Lane (celebrating the slaughter of French invaders in 1377) changed to the less ghoulish Trafalgar Road following the victorious sea battle.

Slovens Bush Turnpike on the Wroxall to Ventnor road at the junction leading to Rew Farm.

Mead Hole, the main anchorage in the sixteenth century, preceding Cowes, was notorious for smugglers.

Elephant Hole and Cripple Path – part of the Undercliff. Elephant Hole, a cavern, was probably used as a depository for contraband while Cripple Path is said to be part of a pilgrims way en route to a holy well at Whitwell.

Two areas of barren land at Staplers Heath are known as Smallgrains Farm and Mount Misery. Shrewdly, Queen Victoria sold them off when they became part of her estate.

Banger's Whistle – on the Newport to Yarmouth road – was probably named for the sound of the train approaching Watchingwell Halt.

Chiddles – the White Horse Inn at Whitwell was once called Chiddles Cottage. There is also a Chiddles Farm at Alverstone.

Shiney Brick – Shiny Brick Lane leads to the Hermitage near Chale.

Gallibury Hump is a round barrow on the outskirts of Brighstone Forest.

Eaglehead and Bloodstone copses are at Ashey.

Bare Ass Bottom is land to the south of Hulverstone Farm – its origin is left to the readers' imagination.

Annual Holidays

In the eighteenth century potatoes were traditionally planted on Good Friday, being the only holiday given to poor people, apart from Christmas Day.

Gold Fever

Blackgang experienced a mini gold rush as men panned for treasure on the shingle of the beach – until it was discovered that the coins had been washed ashore from a wreck.

Coal Mining

Sufficient deposits of lignite coal were identified at Whitecliff Bay to justify brief commercial mining. The coal however was difficult to burn and sulphurous so the mining was short-lived. Another good idea up in flames.

The Island's oldest man-made structure is now beneath the sea. Some 8,000 years old, divers discovered evidence of planking installed by islanders at Bouldnor Cliff.

Unfortunate Loss of Income?

Revenue collected on the Island dropped dramatically when America won the War of Independence. Until that time, trading ships bound from the States to the Continent called at Cowes to pay duty on the cargo. It was a nice little earner. Over 8,000 tons of rice passed through, plus tobacco, indigo, pitch, tar and turpentine in 1781. The cargo also included slaves, perhaps bound for domestic service. Did some of them end up in the bigger Island houses? There was controversy as to whether slavery existed in Britain and anyone landed here was technically free, but London's coffee houses frequently carried notices seeking 'runaway slaves'. In any case, where was a stranger in a strange land to go? Slavery was abolished in Britain in 1807.

The Lord Giveth

In March 1837, following an inquest on Mr Thomas Taylor who died suddenly, the verdict was that he had died 'by visitation of God.'

Famous Island Buildings Destroyed by Fire

Freshwater Windmill, destroyed in 1840, is now the site of a school.

The Needles Hotel burned down 1910.

The Sandrock Hotel, servicing a spa and visited by Queen Victoria, was consumed by fire in 1984, the site was then cleared for housing.

St Lawrence Hall, retirement home of John Earl Jellicoe, first Lord of the Admiralty, met an untimely end in 1951 when fire engulfed it and the 10-acre site was converted into a housing estate.

Mew Langton Brewery was demolished 1979. The brewery probably dated from the seventeenth century but was definitely in operation by 1815. Sold to Whitbreads, they closed the site. A fire in the grade 2 listed malt house allowed its demolition to be replaced with a housing complex.

Hazards House, built about 1684, was one of Newport's oldest buildings. Purchased by the council it was hoped that it would be protected, but a fire in the 1960s damaged it sufficiently to enable demolition, replacing it with the Island's ugliest building – the County Hall extension.

Fernhill was a fine eighteenth-century gentleman's residence at Wootton. Passing through various owners, it was in the process of conversion to smaller houses when a fire consumed it in 1938.

The Theatre Royal, Ryde's oldest theatre and latterly cinema, was destroyed by fire in 1961. Dorothy Jordan, mistress of King William IV, and Ellen Terry were among its performers. A NatWest Bank now occupies the site.

Other Sad Losses

Steephill Castle, a gothic, turreted monolith built by Mr John Hambrough and sold to rich American industrialist John Morgan Richards, suffered various incarnations as a hotel and school before fire regulations saw it demolished in 1963 to be replaced by housing.

East Cowes Castle was built by architect John Nash as his retirement home. Visitors included the Prince of Wales and J.M.W. Turner. On Nash's death it was sold to pay his debts. Commissioned by the military during the war, it was neglected and demolished in the 1960s, and was replaced by a housing estate.

Appley Towers, overlooking Ryde, was a fine mock Elizabethan mansion occupied by the Hutt dynasty and built by local architect Thomas

Hellyer. When owned by shipping magnate Hedworth Williamson, it was visited several times by Queen Mary. It survived a fire in 1910 but was demolished in the 1960s. The site is now a leisure area.

Totland Bay Hotel was part of an ambitious development turning a fishing hamlet into an upmarket seaside resort. Attractive red-brick villas with uniform tiles blossomed in the area. The hotel was built at the same time as the pier, to encourage day-trippers. Used by the military during the war, the hotel never recovered and stringent safety regulations ensured its destruction, being replaced by a block of flats. At the time of writing, the pier hangs on by a thread.

2

SHIPWRECKS, SMUGGLERS, PIRATES AND SPIES

SOME WRECKS THAT ROCKED THE ISLAND

At least 4,000 ships have come to grief around the Island's coast, with many others unrecorded. A few particular wrecks still inspire the public imagination.

Mary Rose was the pride of Henry VIII's navy, named for his sister. Following his break with the Church of Rome, Catholic nations viewed England as the enemy and in 1545 King Francis I of France anchored off the Island, ready to do battle. King Henry watched proceedings from Southsea Castle. The *Mary Rose* prepared to attack when disaster struck. Her gun ports being open, as she came about, water flooded into the vessel and she sank. Only forty of the 700 aboard survived. The following year peace with France was agreed.

The *Royal George* flagship, beloved of the navy, helped to secure British victory during the Seven Years War. In 1782 she was called to defend Gibraltar from threatened Spanish attack. Needing minor repairs she was taken into Portsmouth and, rather than work in a dry dock, she was tilted so that the damaged area would be above the water line. As the carpenters worked, her hundred cannon and all supplies on board were moved to one side. Apart from the crew of 820 men, friends, family and local merchants delivering goods were all on board. Perhaps inevitably she tilted too far and began to take on water. By the time the captain was informed and ordered that she should be righted, it was too late. *Royal George* capsized and 1,065 people perished. Many were washed ashore at Ryde and a memorial plaque is installed along the Esplanade.

Eurydice was a sight to behold: an old fashioned sailing ship used to train cadets in a now dying art. On 24 March 1878, people taking the air at Ventnor stopped to admire her, scudding along at speed, for already the more prosaic steam ships were taking her place. Out of the blue a storm blew up and the walkers ran for cover. When they ventured out, *Eurydice* had disappeared. In that short time she sank, drowning 317 crew and cadets. There followed the gruesome task of raising the vessel with most of the drowned men still on board. Other bodies were washed ashore along the coast. *Eurydice* was towed to Sandown Bay and the waterlogged, rotting corpses were brought out, the mission hindered by sightseers, not least a party aboard the royal yacht *Britannia,* where the Prince of Wales had brought his family to watch.

Fourteen unidentified bodies were buried on the Island, seven at Shanklin cemetery and seven at Christchurch in Sandown. The cause of the accident was never satisfactorily explained but bizarrely, the only two survivors were charged with losing their ship! They had been rescued with three others by a passing boat, the *Emma,* her captain was also blamed for causing death because being a temperance ship he had no brandy on board to revive them.

In November 1859, the *Lelia of London,* carrying a cargo of sponges from the West Indies, went ashore between Blackgang and Rocken End. For several days, the beach was littered with sponges, a novel but probably irrelevant addition to the bathing habits of the locals.

The barque *Cedrene,* carrying 191 convicts and forty-three overseers, ran aground off the back of the Wight on 2 April 1862. The men on board were returning from the West Indies following transportation and had now completed their sentences. All were safely brought ashore and guided to Brighstone where, no doubt celebrating their freedom and survival, they promptly drank the pub dry. A punch-up ensued and men from the barracks at Parkhurst had to be summoned to restore order.

In the same year another ship's crew was less lucky. The *Lotus* was en route from Demarera carrying a cargo of sugar and rum to London. She was caught in a storm on 18 October and quickly broke up. Of the fourteen people on board, only two survived. The incident caused

a furore for it was claimed that the locals were more interested in the cargo than the crew. Sugar, ships' timbers and rum was carried away and people were drunk on the beach. Whether more could have been done, who knows? The unfortunate seamen were buried at Chale.

In the opening year of the First World War the *Delmira* was mined by a U-Boat 4 miles off Shanklin. According to local longshoreman Clifford Rayner, on board were about 4,000 men of the West Africa Labour Corps, en route to France, who nearly all perished. If so, the tragedy was a terrible but well kept secret. Perhaps he had confused the event with the 1917 sinking of the *Mendi* with about 600 men from South Africa on board, bound for war work in France. She was sawn in half by a ship, the *Darro*, that failed to give assistance to the men in the water, most of whom died. The captain of the *Darro* was charged with travelling too fast in fog and lost his licence for a year. Racial prejudice was blamed for his failure to help the stricken men. The site of the sinking of the *Mendi* is now a recognised war grave.

In 1918, the world's largest oil tanker, the American steamship *O.B. Jennings,* collided with the SS *War Knight,* damaging both ships. The

War Knight ran aground in Watcombe Bay and the *Jennings* was towed to Sandown Bay. Both ships burned for fourteen days as huge amounts of oil leaked onto the beaches. Eventually the *Jennings* was patched up and set sail for America, but half way across the Atlantic she hit a mine and sank.

Perhaps the best remembered shipwreck is the *Clarendon*. On 27 August 1836 she set sail from St Kitts carrying a cargo of rum and molasses. Her voyage took six weeks and on 10 October she was within spitting distance of Southampton when a gale blew up. In the darkness, *Clarendon* ran ashore. Within five minutes she broke up ,littering the beach with cargo and timbers. Rescuers were helpless to reach her and twenty-five people drowned. What shocked the public was the death on board of a naval lieutenant named Shore, his wife and four daughters, the youngest just nine-months-old. Most of the crew was buried at Chale but the Shores seem to have been interred at Newport.

The burial ground at Church Litten is now a park. Timbers from *Clarendon* were used to build the Clarendon Inn at Shanklin, only recently demolished. The pub, the White Mouse at Chale, changed its name in memory of the stricken vessel. The tragedy underlined the need for a warning light and so St Catherine's lighthouse was commissioned.

SMUGGLING – THE ISLAND'S OLDEST PROFESSION?

Rudyard Kipling may well have had the Island in mind when he wrote his poem, 'A Smuggler's Song'. The opening lines convey the sense that smugglers could be dangerous men: 'If you wake at midnight, and hear a horse's feet. Don't go drawing back the blind, or looking in the street...' At its height, two-thirds of Island sailors and fishermen were reckoned to be involved in smuggling. Those who were not turned a blind eye.

While the trade was synonymous with brandy and tobacco, one of the Island's early preoccupations was with salt, for some 800 years processed around the coast, the name Salterns and Saltings being a reminder. To extract it, seawater was dried out during the summer months and then boiled in pans to form crystals. The industry was hit by a salt tax introduced in 1693 and smuggling became rife.

'Salt Officers' were employed at Shalfleet, Yarmouth, Newtown, Thorley, Elmsworth (East of Newtown), Nettlestone, Cowes, Freshwater, Calbourne and Thorness. The smuggling trade ceased when the salt tax was finally removed in 1824.

In 1777, William Arnold, father of Thomas Arnold of Rugby School fame, was appointed Collector of Customs for the Island, based at East Cowes. At the time it was reported that 'Smugglers in general are becoming more daring than ever, and more frequently assemble in numbers carrying arms and in disguise. Instances occur every year of officers being wounded, beaten, opposed and obstructed in the execution of their duty...' Customs officers augmented their salaries by receiving a share of the profits from selling off contraband goods – a great incentive scheme. Many local people were sympathetic to the smugglers, even lending a hand in an emergency. A house with a ship carved into the stone indicated that a smuggler could call on help within.

Although spirits were the main contraband, the high duty on tea meant that it was also sought after. If discovered, the felons were charged three times its value. At Brook in 1825, Mr and Mrs Mark Butcher were relieved of 6lbs of tea and charged £9.

Men who made their living from the sea and supplemented their income by smuggling were frequently punished by serving their sentences in the navy. In 1825 Frederick Adams, Reuben Coleman, John Calloway and William Southall were caught aboard the boat *Sylph* with twenty tubs of spirits and eighty-four kegs of brandy and were sent to serve aboard the HMS *Victory* for five years.

Sailing from France in March 1878 with a ship loaded with barrels of brandy, lifeboat-man Rufus Cotton and his crew came upon the wreck of the *Eurydice*. They were unable to help because every available space on their craft was filled with illegal barrels. Later, they must have pondered if they might not have saved lives by sacrificing their cargo.

Many customs officers were employed patrolling the coast, collecting excise duty, seizing contraband and prosecuting smugglers. Inadvertently, the smugglers had spawned a job creation scheme.

Being an Excise Man often proved dangerous. In 1716, Richard Young was a mate on the customs yacht *Greenhill*, relaying anything suspicious to the Customs Office at Cowes. During a confrontation a smuggler named William Harris killed Young and fled the scene. His description was circulated but there is no evidence that he was caught.

Fifty pounds reward was offered in July 1804 for the apprehension of three men who bludgeoned customs men Daniel Dore and George Grainger. The officers had seized forty casks of spirits and temporarily stored them at Bembridge, but the felons broke in and stole them back, attacking the officers in the process

There was a nasty attack at Totland Bay when a customs man was stoned to death confronting a crew landing a smuggled cargo. Worse, at Alum Bay, a brave but foolish officer tried to prevent a craft from taking to the sea by hanging on to the stern. Refusing to let go, a crewman struck him with a billhook, severing his hands.

Sometimes an injury was accidental. Following a fall at Chine Avenue in Shanklin, a coastguard landed on his pistol, which went off and: 'which had completely misplaced his heart and driven one lung into a small lump.' Not surprisingly the poor man died three days later. He was buried at Brading.

The customs men were not the only innocent victims. In the churchyard at Binstead stands a memorial stone to sixty-four-year-old Thomas Sivell, who died on 15 June 1785 when he was mistaken for a smuggler and shot. In fact he was innocently plying his trade in the Solent. His distraught wife erected a tombstone, warning that, 'All you that pass, pray look and see; How soon my life was took from me; By those officers as you hear; They spill'd my blood that was so dear; But God is Good is Just and True, And will reward to each their due.'

Contraband was picked up in all parts of the Island and hidden in unlikely places; weighted and tied to lobster pots at sea, in coves and caves around the shore, in cellars, pigsties, hedges and even graves. If caught the goods were seized, including the ship, and the perpetrators were sometimes punished with a fine but if they couldn't pay up, then it was prison and hard labour.

Ann Sothcott was originally fined £4 for concealing smuggled goods but when she failed to pay she was sent to prison.

Contraband seized was put up for sale and it was not unusual to see items advertised in newspapers. On 22 February 1802, forty-six half barrels of Red Herrings were auctioned at East Cowes Customs House, while a fully equipped boat known as the *Resolution* was offered for sale at the Fountain Hotel, West Cowes in February 1800.

Things did not always go to plan. On 10 June 1869 the *Isle of Wight Times* reported the appearance at the County Court of George Colenut on two charges of smuggling ashore 125 gallons of spirits and of being illegally aboard a certain vessel on the night in question. The coastguard had witnessed the boat landing between 1 a.m. and 2 a.m. and a total of forty-two tubs were later found on the beach near Luccombe Chine. The boat contained some rope that was similar to that wrapped around the tubs. This being the only evidence and the fact that Colenut was a fisherman and therefore likely to be at sea and to carry rope, the magistrates took no time in dismissing the case.

A tax on cloth landed Thomas Symode, the rector of All Saints' Church at Freshwater, in court, accused of smuggling woollen cloth. This local, rather rough cloth was known as Kersey and Symonde was caught red-handed in 1394 but claimed 'benefit of clergy,' by which ministers of the Church could not be tried by secular law. At some point, a wag recorded the event in verse, beginning: 'Ye Rector of Freshwater (sad to relate), Was dogg'd and collared at Ye Red Lion Inne. A matter of conflict betwixte Church and State, He was snuggled, in smuggled woolle next Ye Skinne...'

ROYAL SHENANIGANS

Queen Victoria must have been outraged to learn that following her visit to Antwerp in 1852, an inspection of the royal yacht by customs officers revealed widespread smuggling of tobacco. The felony came to light when an Antwerp paper, the *Journal de Commerce*, reported on the benefits of the royal visit where some 5,000lbs of tobacco had been purchased from local shops. On searching the royal yacht *Victoria and Albert*, 80lbs of the contraband tobacco was found and seized. Four of the crew from the squadron were later found in possession of illegal tobacco. They were Samuel White, William Long, Robert Layton and George Cox. The tobacco was purchased for 4*d* a lb in Antwerp and had a market value of 3/6*d* a lb in England.

The royal yacht long remained under suspicion and Customs kept an eye on her for decades. They were finally rewarded in 1887, the year of the Queen's Jubilee, when the vessel was lying in Cowes Road while Her Majesty took a holiday at Osborne. Deciding on a night out, some of the crew set out for Portsmouth but were stopped and searched by Cowes customs men, producing a haul of 40lbs of cigars and tobacco. The seven crewmembers were collected by the yacht's captain, Fullerton, and held on board to await trial. How Queen Victoria must have suffered!

Operation Eyeful

Smuggling is not a thing of the past. In July 2002, six men were arrested having smuggled 879lbs of cocaine onto the Island. It had a street value of £90 million. Sailing from the tiny island of Bequia in the Caribbean, their intention was to land at Orchard's Bay, where they already had a house to use as a base. They were foiled, however, by the weather, being forced instead into Windy Bay, a mile away. They then proceeded to lug the contraband up the cliffs to their intended destination. It was all in vain for the Island coastguards had been alerted and 150 customs officers awaited their arrival. The trial lasted for six months and the ringleader, Michael Tyrell, was jailed for twenty-six years. A collective sentence of ninety years was passed on the men.

Yarmouth saw a surprise discovery in 2010 when cocaine to the value of £8 million was identified. A seaman apparently emptying his lobster pots mistakenly pulled up a pot belonging to someone else. Attached to it was a holdall. Thinking that it may have been accidentally lost at sea and become entangled with the pot, he opened it to try and identify the owner. Inside were bags of white powder. The police and coastguards were informed and the lucrative trade uncovered.

PIRATES

In the seventeenth century raids along the English coast by Barbary Corsairs resulted in many kidnaps. In 1694, Ann Newland of the Isle of Wight left the sad provision in her will for 'My grandson John Smith' who was held as a slave. She bequeathed him 'half of all I have in the world,' either to pass to him on his return home or to be used to purchase his freedom.

Parliamentary proceedings of 1695 reported that pirates from Algiers had taken men and women making hay on the Island. The kidnappers had declared that they liked English women so well that they had captured one each.

William Oakley, kidnapped off the island along with his ship the *Mary* in 1639, recounted his days as a slave, sold in the open market at Algiers and eventually making his escape by building a canvas ship and rowing for six days until he reached Majorca.

Jack Ward was a British seaman licensed by Queen Elizabeth to take Spanish ships for the Crown; when James I revoked the licence he turned his hand to piracy. He changed his name to Yusuf Reis and based his operations in Tunis. In 1603 he sailed to the Island and captured the *Violet* in the belief that she was full of Spanish treasure, but found that she was empty. He rarely spoke without swearing and was known to be drunk from morning to night. He died from the plague in 1622.

SPIES

The British authorities were always on the lookout for spies. In 1789, as revolution flared in France, they arrested the artist George Morland, at a house in Yarmouth. Morland was on the run from his creditors, and to keep one step ahead, he was frequently on the move. At Yarmouth some drawings were seized, suspected of being plans for a French invasion, but witnesses came forward as to his 'good' character and the magistrates released him. Morland spent his island sojourn drinking and socialising with fishermen in local taverns, paying his way by dashing off a painting for the price of a drink.

Dorothy O'Grady, a landlady living in Sandown, was the only woman to be sentenced to death for spying during the Second World War. Frequently seen walking her dog in forbidden areas, she was arrested when she tried to cut some telegraph wires. Her trial was heard *in camera* and she was sentenced to hang but the sentence was later reduced to fourteen years in gaol. Released in 1950, Dorothy returned to the Island, claiming that she had been suffering from some kind of 'kink' and that she only wanted attention. The general consensus was that she was 'dotty'. Shortly after her papers were released they were withdrawn again, but those who saw them concluded that she was the most dangerous and cunning Nazi spy ever recruited. She died in a nursing home at Lake.

Among the prisoners in Parkhurst gaol in 1913 was William Klare, 'one of the cleverest spies in the German Foreign Service.' Klare was a dentist working in Portsmouth and developed various friendships with dockyard personnel. One of his contacts, Levi Rosenthal, was in fact a government spy and when he was offered $1,000 by Klare to borrow a naval book, Rosenthal reported him. He was sentenced to five years for spying.

Spying was never more rife on the Island than in 1648, when Charles I was imprisoned at Carisbrooke Castle. Revelling in the intrigue, the king enjoyed an exciting secret correspondence with the help of his minders, men implicitly trusted by the harassed governor Robert Hammond. Humiliatingly information regularly reached Hammond from London reporting the latest escape attempt that had taken place under his nose. Numerous, supposedly loyal men were expelled from the castle, the names Ashburnham, Berkeley, Burrows, Cresset, Dowcett, Firebrace, Legge and Osborn going down in history. It also seems that double agents were at work – but these were never identified

3

POSH PEOPLE

THE ROYALS

King Alfred the Great's mother, Queen Osburga, was born at her father's manor of Arreton in about AD 810. Her father, Oslac, married her to Æthelwulf of Wessex and her son Alfred was born in 849.

Lady Isabella di Fortibus was the last independent ruler of the Isle of Wight (*see* Chapter 5 – Girl Power).

King Henry VI personally crowned his boyhood playmate Henry Beauchamp King of the Island in 1444. It is doubtful if the new king ever visited his kingdom and two years after his 'enthronement', he died at the age of twenty-one. The Island passed back to the Tudors.

Henry VIII paid a visit to Richard Worsley at Appuldurcombe House in 1538. He had a particular fondness for Richard's father James, who had served him as a paige, knighting him and giving him the captaincy of the Island. At the time of Henry's visit he was still in mourning for the death of his third wife, Jane Seymour. Whether he found temporary consolation locally, who knows!

The year after King Charles was beheaded his children, Prince Henry Duke of York and Princess Elizabeth, arrived at Carisbrooke Castle. She was fifteen and he was eight. After only a few weeks, Elizabeth, who was a weakly child, caught a fever and died. She was hurriedly buried in Newport. Her remains came to light 300 years later when the church was rebuilt and Queen Victoria appointed the sculptor Carlo Marochetti to carve an unrealistic statue of the 'beautiful princess'. In reality the poor girl suffered from rickets and was badly deformed. Prince Henry remained for two years before being released to join his brother, the future King Charles II. He died at the age of twenty-one.

THE QUEEN VIC

Queen Victoria fell in love with the splendid isolation of Osborne Bay near Cowes, with far reaching implications for the sleepy Island. She bought the estate – consisting of 342 acres and a nice Georgian house – from Lady Isabella Blachford, daughter of the 3rd Duke of Grafton and descended from King Charles II. Her husband, Robert Pope Blachford, had grown rich on the profits of slave trading. Prince Albert agreed to the purchase but wanted more land and extended the search to neighbouring Barton and Alverstone Farms, adding Heathfield, Kingston and Truckles plus an assortment of land, cottages and copses.

Victoria was looking for something intimate and secluded and to her eyes they had found it. The original Osborne House was knocked down and a three-storey building set in 1,727 acres emerged. She was delighted with 'dear, modest, unpretentious Osborne.' The royal family could now drive on 20 miles of road without leaving their estate.

When Queen Victoria went to the new church at Whippingham, she promptly offered to pay £10 for the organist to have music lessons!

A Case of Mistaken Identity!
In 1848 the Queen and Prince Albert were advised to decamp to Osborne for their safety. In London the Chartists claimed to have collected 6 million signatures demanding electoral reform and things looked like turning ugly. Today their demands sound reasonable enough but they sent terror through those in power, asking for universal male suffrage, no property qualifications for MPs, secret ballots, payment for MPs, equal electoral districts and annual parliaments. Queen Victoria fully expected to be murdered. In June her worst fears were aroused. Osborne was put on a state of alert following reports that a mob had been seen gathering at Cowes. Like some medieval manor, the servants were armed with sticks and poles, the crew from the Queen's escort ship *Fairy*, moored at Cowes, arrived complete with weapons and a battalion from Parkhurst Barracks gave a creditable impression of the cavalry. Finally news reached Osborne that the crisis was over. The Chartists turned out to be a group of 'Oddfellows' enjoying a day out!

From Cradle to Grave?

The royal family provided much work locally but they were careful not to pay more than the going rate. Albert insisted on building workers' cottages in keeping with their status and the old and widowed were 'looked after.'

On 4 February 1864, the Queen and her half sister Princess Feodora of Leinengen opened the new Whippingham School, designed by her beloved (and now deceased) Albert. She also gave land for a new cemetery at Kingston.

The Silly Season

The activities of the Queen and her family were naturally of great interest to the locals but the Isle of Wight County press must have been seriously short of news in August 1891, when it reported that 'The Queen has driven several times through Newport during the past week.'

When Queen Victoria visited Alum Bay she was presented with some 'chimney piece' ornaments, glass objects filled with local coloured sand, thus starting a fashion that continues today.

Queen Victoria's favourite grandson, the future Kaiser Wilhelm of Germany, frequently visited. He was by her side when she died at Osborne House.

Following the Queen's death, between 1903 and 1921 part of Osborne House was used as a naval college. Among the pupils were Victoria's great grandsons the future, George VI and Edward VIII.

King George V took up sailing, entering with gusto into the events during Cowes week aboard the royal yacht *Britannia*. So enamoured of the vessel did he become that before he died he ordered that *Britannia* should be buried at sea. She was scuttled off St Catherine's Point.

There was excitement at Sandown in April 1891 when Queen Victoria's favourite son, Arthur, Duke of Connaught, came to inspect the militia. Unfortunately the Duke's carriage was smashed to smithereens when his horses were frightened by the exuberance of the local band and bolted. Quick thinking Lady Barnaholt offered the shaken Duke the use of her donkey cart but he was not impressed. Eventually a shandrydan, a two wheeled, hooded chaise was procured and the event progressed. (The word shandrydan can mean any old fashioned, decrepit form of transport.) Clearly unfazed, the Duke later wrote to the commander of the band to say how much he had enjoyed the day.

None of Queen Victoria's children were born on the Island but they all spent part of their childhood here. With a seriously upmarket Wendy house known as 'Swiss Cottage,' a chalet imported from Switzerland, the princes and princesses had their own gardens. They grew flowers (roses, lilies, pinks) fruit (strawberries, gooseberries, currants, raspberries) and vegetables, (asparagus, artichokes, potatoes, turnips, cabbages, onions, carrots, parsnips and lettuce). When Vicky, the Crown Princess of Prussia (the eldest child and favourite of her father) moved to Germany to be married, she ordered her vegetables to be sent each summer from Osborne to Berlin.

Queen Victoria finally found consolation after Prince Albert's death in the company of two unlikely men. John Brown, a Scottish ghillie had served Prince Albert in Scotland and in a desperate attempt to shake the Queen out of her torpor, he was brought to Osborne. No doubt his presence reminded her of happier times and initially it had the desired effect. Growing increasingly dependent on him however, her family became alarmed, relying on their mother's poor, harassed secretary Sir Henry Ponsonby to sort it out. The 'problem' was finally resolved by Brown's death in 1883. Queen Victoria was allegedly buried with his photo in her coffin.

In a mammoth effort to interest the Queen in new horizons, Prime Minister Benjamin Disraeli engineered her appointment as Empress of India. For some time Victoria had been miffed because, while she was a Queen, her eldest daughter Vicky was an Empress. Now Victoria was an Empress too and she took great interest in her new territories. Into her life came her second 'friend', Abdul Karim, a young servant brought into her court largely for ceremonial reasons. The Queen was instantly entranced by his dark good looks and exotic clothes, appointing him as a secretary to teach her Hindustani. No doubt a degree of jealousy and racism came into play and, as to be expected, the more her court objected, the more Victoria clung to 'dear Abdul,' installing him and his family in Albert Cottage on the Osborne Estate. His claim to be the son of a scholar turned out to be slightly misleading – his father was in fact a hospital orderly. Endless rows ensued, frequent tantrums from Her Majesty, and Abdul indeed seemed to bully her. When Victoria died, the first thing her son Edward did was to ship Abdul back to India.

After being installed as Empress of India, the royal coach, usually pulled by four grey horses, was to be seen on the Island with an additional escort of Scottish and Indian servants in traditional dress.

In 1909, Tsar Nicholas II visited the Island to review the fleet.

Whale Knocks off Queen's Hat!
Whilst visiting Blackgang, Queen Mary, wife of King George V, took a walk inside the skeleton of the great whale on display. The creature's jawbone caught her hat, knocking it off to the consternation of the hosts. The offending piece of bone was immediately sawn off. The fin whale measuring, 19m, had washed up off the Needles in 1842. It was put up for auction and enterprising Mr Alexander Dabell bought it as a tourist attraction. Its skeleton remains on display at Blackgang today.

Queen Mary was a reluctant sailor and while her husband scooted around the Island on the water, she visited her friend Sir Hedworth Williamson at Appley Towers in Ryde. A lookout tower, a quaint folly at the water's edge, was allegedly erected so that she could enjoy the spectacle of naval reviews – from the land.

In 1912 Princess Beatrice, Victoria's youngest daughter and dutiful companion, moved from Osborne House to Carisbrooke Castle after her brother Edward gave Osborne to the nation. Beatrice once showed a rare moment of stubbornness: with the support of her sisters, she had been allowed to marry the dashing Prince Henry Battenberg, on condition that the pair remained with the Queen. Henry, created Governor of the Island, soon grew bored and escaped to the excitement of the Ashanti Wars.

Unfortunately, he caught a fever, died and was shipped home, to be buried at St Mildred's in Whippingham, where a chapel was dedicated to his memory. Beatrice became the new Governor of the Island, living at Carisbrooke Castle until her death in 1944. She was widowed even longer than her mother.

SOME ISLAND MEMORIALS ERECTED TO QUEEN VICTORIA

The Queen's Golden Jubilee, 1887
A clock tower was added to John Nash's Guildhall in Newport.

An ornate clock tower was erected on Shanklin seafront.

Lord Gort donated land for a Jubilee Recreation Ground at East Cowes.

A drinking fountain at Wootton, originally stood at the bottom of the hill but was later moved to the garden of No.80 High Street, where it is visible from the road.

The Queen's Diamond Jubilee, 1897
The Victoria Recreation Ground at Newport opened on land donated by the dashingly named Tankerville Chamberlayne MP and was opened by Princess Beatrice.

A bridge in Wroxall village was built along the main road.

The children's Ward at Ryde County Hospital marked the Jubilee but is now demolished. The Queen's bust from the hospital is in the waiting area at St Mary's Hospital. The brick and stone archway was moved to the Square.

The Queen's Death

The Victoria monument at St James's Square in Newport was erected in 1903 following the Queen's death at Osborne. It was designed by the Island's favourite architect, Percy Stone.

The Island is littered with roads and avenues named either Queen's or Victoria.

Royal Visitors

The following Royals were known to pop over to the Island:

King Alfred fought the Vikings from Brading Haven in 897; In 1013 Ethelred the Unready spent Christmas on the Island; In 1173 Queen Eleanor of Acquitaine was allegedly imprisoned in Quarr Abbey. She might even have been buried there – in a gold coffin! In 1214 King John was at Yarmouth; In 1348 Edward III set sail from St Helens to invade Normandy; In 1648 Charles I spent an uncomfortable year at Carisbrooke Castle trying to get away. Charles II made several visits to the Island, at least one of them giving him a bumpy ride. The Parish Register for Niton records that on 1 July 1675 Charles II King of Great Britain, France and Ireland etc., came safely ashore at Puckaster, after he had endured a great and dangerous storm at sea. One of his visits was to confer a knighthood on Sir Edward Worsley, who had helped his father during his failed escapes, and also to visit his friend the Governor Sir Robert Holmes. In 1890, the Prince of Naples, member of the House of Savoy, visited Osborne along with the Duke and Duchess of Connaught.

Napoleon III and the Empress Eugenie and also Elizabeth, Empress of Austria, stayed at Steephill Castle in Ventnor.

In 1987, Queen Elizabeth II visited the Island to commemorate the second centenary of the First Fleet sailing to Australia. The ceremony took place in St Thomas's Church and nine pigeons then living in the building were shot.

Prince Charles, Princess Margaret, Princess Alexandra, Princes William and Harry have all visited to carry out ceremonial functions.

Other Big Wigs

In 1642, in the heat of the battle of Edgehill, Sir Faithful Fortescue famously changed sides. Having served the king in Ireland, he was then assigned to the Earl of Essex, who, at the outbreak of war, joined the parliamentary forces, leaving Sir Faithful on what he considered to be the wrong side. In mid battle he arranged to go over to the Royalists but unfortunately, his men forgot that they were wearing the orange sashes of the Parliamentarians and seventeen were shot by their new allies.

After going into exile with King Charles II, Sir Faithful returned to London at the Restoration. On the outbreak of plague in 1665 he retired to the Island, living at Bowcombe Manor. He died in 1666 and is buried in St Mary's Church at Carisbrooke, where his descendant, Thomas, Lord Clermont, put up a brass plaque in his honour.

Sir Thomas Fleming, Lord Chief Justice during the reign of James I, was one of the judges who sentenced Guy Fawkes to death. His name is kept alive through the Binstead pub the Fleming Arms.

In 1864, George Stephenson, the railway genius, gave a cast-iron drinking fountain and an area known as The Green to Cowes for the town's pleasure. Upstaging him, in 1926 a second, stolid fountain was donated by the townspeople to honour Edward Prince of Wales, the future Edward VIII. They also changed the name of the area to Prince's Green. What would George Stephenson have thought of that?

The Earl of Yarborough, a sailing fanatic who inaugurated Cowes Week, died appropriately aboard his yacht the *Kestral* at Vigo in Spain.

Sir John Oglander, seventeenth-century commentator on all things local, tells that with his friend the Earl of Southampton, he and thirty to forty other 'knights and gentlemen' met twice weekly on St George's Down to play bowls, cards and tuck into an 'ordinary' (a meal).

In his time as Chancellor of the Exchequer, James Callaghan had a holiday home at Alma Cottage in Wellow.

Alfred Lord Tennyson, mindful of his status as Poet Laureate, dutifully trotted out poems for royal occasions, including the wedding of Princess Beatrice and the Queen Victoria's Diamond Jubilee. He took up residence at Farringford House, Freshwater.

THE FOLLOWING PEOPLE DIED ON THE ISLAND

Queen Victoria died at Osborne on, 23 January 1901. Her body was ceremoniously moved from Osborne to Cowes for onward transmission to Windsor, where she was buried at Frogmore.

Lady Elizabeth Henrietta Cole, seemingly far from home, lies behind railings in Chale churchyard. Her life had an unfortunate beginning. Her mother Elizabeth, daughter of the Duke of Hamilton, had married Edward Smith Stanley, 12th Earl of Derby. Perhaps it was his preference for racehorses that drove her into the arms of John Sackville, 3rd Earl of Dorset, thus producing young Elizabeth. The countess discretely went to Switzerland for the birth. Lord Derby refused to divorce his wife so in name if not reality, Elizabeth was his daughter. At seventeen, she was married off to Stephen Thomas Cole, a wealthy brewer. Stephen died twenty-two years before his wife. In 1851 she was living on her father's estate at Knowsley Hall in Lancashire. How she came to the Isle of Wight remains a mystery.

Lord John George Lambton, or 'Radical Jack' as he was known, was the wealthy land and coal-mine owner in the north-east of England. His second marriage was to Louisa, daughter of the future Prime Minister Lord Grey. Lambton was an enthusiastic reformer and his was a solitary voice advocating universal suffrage in 1832. He served as Governor General of Canada and Ambassador to the court of St Petersburg, pursuing various foreign policies advocated by the government. A combination of fragile health plus the loss of two children, his wife and his mother in short succession, found him increasingly sick and he retired to the Island, where he had a house and a yacht (the *Louisa*) at Cowes. There he died aged forty-three in 1840. His body was returned to his Durham estate for burial.

Emily, Lady Tennyson

Like a creaking gate, Emily Tennyson hung on longer than her husband, outliving him by four years. On his death, Alfred, as Poet Laureate, was whisked off to Poets' Corner at Westminster Abbey. Emily devoted the rest of her life to help write the authorised biography of her husband and when she died was buried at All Saints' Church in Freshwater.

Princess Beatrice, Queen Victoria's youngest daughter, after a lifetime of service as Island Governor, died in 1944. She was buried in the family chapel at Whippingham Church along with her husband, Prince Henry Battenburg.

Prince Louis Mountbatten, great uncle of Prince Phillip, died on the Island in 1917. He is buried at Whippingham Church.

Sir Henry Ponsonby, the Queen's long-suffering secretary, eventually succumbed to the stress of royal service and is buried at Whippingham. Among his many delicate tasks was to act as mediator between the royal children and Her Majesty over the delicate issues of John Brown and the Indian servant Abdul Karim, both of whom the Queen was disturbingly fond.

King of the Cocos Islands, George Clunies Ross the absolute ruler, died at Ventnor in 1909. Cocos had first been discovered 300 years earlier by William Keeling, whose memorial is in Carisbrooke Church.

Cocos-Keeling was colonised by John Clunies Ross, George's grandfather, founding a new population consisting of twenty europeans and 155 East Indians. In 1886, Queen Victoria's government accidentally annexed the island but the Queen gave it back to George in perpetuity. Family members in Britain attended the funeral at Bonchurch and George was embalmed and buried for five years before he was disinterred and shipped back to the Islands. Keeling-Cocos is now administered by Australia.

Lady Margaret Wadham, aunt of Queen Jane Seymour who became the third wife of Henry VIII, lived at Alvington Manor and is buried at St Mary's Carisbrooke. Her husband, Sir Nicholas, was governor of the Island from 1498-1515. Her niece is said to have visited prior to her marriage to Henry VIII.

4

THE GOOD, THE BAD AND THE DODGY

The Good?

For its spiritual welfare the Island was handed over by Caedwalla, the seventh-century invader to St Wilfred, allegedly making it the last place in Britain to accept Christianity. Only St Wilfred's primary school in Ventnor bears his name.

Dem Bones?

On Good Friday the Holy Cross Church at Seaview displays a tiny fragment of wood purported to be part of the holy cross of the crucifixion. All thanks go to St Helen, mother of the Emperor Constantine, who at the age of eighty supervised the erection of a church at Calvary, where fragments of wood and nails were discovered. She gives her name to the neighbouring St Helens.

Hands Off my Congregation!

December 1, 1144 was a big day in Chale when Hugh Gernon donated a church to the village. Alweitus, vicar of St Mary, Carisbrooke, objected, insisting that the congregation were his. Not only must they attend services at Carisbrooke about 7 miles away but also carry their dead to be buried there. Hugh finally agreed to pay Alweitus a percentage of the church's income. The agreement came with warning – anyone violating it, 'let him be accursed.'

Among the eminent deceased of Arreton are Harry Hawles, who fought at the battle of Agincourt, and William Colnet of Combley, who died in 1594 and whose claim to fame is that he was the great nephew of the last Emperor of Constantinople.

All praise to the Revd Legh Richmond, for seven years curate at St Mary's Church, Brading, whose book *Annals of the Poor* has remained in print ever since its publication in 1814. It made two local girls, Elizabeth Wallbridge, the dairyman's daughter at Arreton, and

Jane Squibb, a cottager at Brading, famous. Both girls died young and were unbelievably good. If you like spiritually uplifting tales of virtue in adversity then this is for you.

Not so well remembered is William 'The Negro Servant', whom Richmond baptised. William thanked his lucky stars in having been a slave, for otherwise he would never have found his way to God – everyone is entitled to their opinion.

Holy Relic?
Richmond's surplice hung in the vestry at Brading for years after his departure. The hem was torn and muddy because, walking with a stoop, he kept treading on it. Little by little pieces were cut off and used by local people as bandages for wounds in the belief that something of his goodness might assist the healing process.

On 1 May 1803, a black man known as Orenoco was baptised on the Island, adopting the name John Binstead. A George Binstead later married Harriet Stonestreet at Ryde – a descendent perhaps?

Fun to be at the YMCA?
Christopher Smith, who died on 1 December 1892 at his Blackgang home, had the kudos of having named the YMCA. Retiring to the Island, he married a local spinster and carried on his good works. On the morning of his death he told his wife that he had had 'such a sweet message from the Lord.' After opening his correspondence and while waiting for morning prayers, he was suddenly 'absent from the body [and] present with the Lord.' (Quite an adjustment one would imagine.) He was laid to rest in Chale churchyard.

Speaking Well of the Dead – Plaques extolling the Departed
At St Boniface Church, Bonchurch, Mr Thomas Prickett (1781-1811) surgeon, 'with piety and resignation closed a life of extensive usefulness.'

Catherine Susanna Bull died at Chale on 8 October 1795 'after a short life of exemplary benevolence, died alas!' Levina Luther died on 28 January 1882 and is commended for a 'life passed in the practice of every virtue.'

At St Helens, Ellen Ellison died – 'a Model of a Christian Wife and Woman.'

Insuring Against Damnation?

Richard Serle at Arreton bought a 40-acre farm, the income being used to buy bread for the poor.

John Mann made a similar provision at Northwood and Whippingham. Richard Knight made a yearly gift of a great coat and a pair of breeches to six poor men of Brading to be distributed each October, while six women each received a 12*d* loaf once a month.

The residents of Chale must have been the best educated in the Island for three local gentlemen invested money to ensure the provision of a school and teacher for the poor of the parish.

David Urry of Freshwater gave income from his lands for the instruction of the children while Dr Culme, rector of Freshwater, left £23 in his will to buy clothes for poor children.

The Revd Edward Worsley in 1702 left £20 towards building a school at Gatcombe, where reading and learning the Catechism was to be taught and a schoolmistress employed.

Lady Ann Worsley supported the founding of a Grammar School at Godshill, originally dated 1615.

At Newchurch William Bowles left £100, the interest to be given to the deserving poor – the vicar to decide who qualified.

Keeping up the tradition, in 1821, Lady Barrington of Swainston 'most generously bestowed 400 coats, 80 jackets and 1,000 faggots on the poor'.

Not to be outdone, Lady Cottle of Ningwood Manor donated chairs to the older residents of Newbridge. Her husband Thomas, vicar of Shalfleet, had a stained-glass window installed in his honour. He died in 1895 aged ninety.

On his death the Revd Benjamin Holmes left £400 to be invested and on St John's Day to purchase Bibles and Testaments for the scholars of Freshwater. The residue was to be spent on loaves. (Bread or Bible anyone?)

The Nonconformists

The Island experienced an upsurge in nonconformist worship resulting in a wealth of chapels bearing the name Bible Christian, Primitive Methodist and Wesleyan. On 1 November 1735, John and Charles Wesley arrived at Cowes. Whether they intended to stay is uncertain but bad weather drove them ashore and it was not until 10 December that they left, setting out for America. A series of preachers, many of them women, came to bring their message. Miss O'Brien, who travelled to Wellow where she preached to a large congregation in a barn, could find no one to give her a bed for the night so she stayed at the Nelson – and she a teetotal lady!

To Turn or to Burn?

Sir John Cheke of Mottistone threw in his lot with Lady Jane Gray, being Secretary of State during her nine-day reign. Imprisoned by Queen Mary he faced the choice of turning to Catholicism or burning at the stake. He chose life but at a cost, depressed at the thought of denying his faith. He died in 1557 aged forty-three.

What's in a Name?

Do not confuse Cardel Goodman, seventh-century rector of Freshwater, with his son Cardel 'Scum' Goodman, actor, murderer, failed assassin and all round rogue, who fled to Paris with a pension – provided he did not come back!

The Ultimate Sacrifice

An Elizabethan Act of Parliament made it illegal for Catholic priests to come into England. Robert Anderton and William Marsden were captured at Cowes on 25 April 1586 as their ship sheltered from a storm. Their undoing was that they were overheard praying for deliverance. The trial took place at Winchester Assizes and the condemned men were returned to the Island, where they were hanged, drawn and quartered. On 15 December 1929, the Pope beatified both men in Rome. In 1933 their bones were reputedly discovered at Arreton Down.

CHURCHES DEDICATED TO
UNUSUAL SAINTS

St Rhadegund (Whitwell) was the sixth-century wife of Clothar the Frank, a brutal Thuringian king. When she ran away, a field of oats sprang up around her, hiding her. At Constantinople she acquired a fragment of the holy cross and also a finger of St Mamas of Cappadocia. Rhadegund was canonised in the ninth century.

St Olave (Gatcombe) was king and later patron saint of Norway, baptised at Rouen and credited with establishing the basic code of Christianity in Norway; he was beatified in 1031.

St Blasius (Shanklin) also known as St Blaise, was clubbed and beheaded for his faith. Being attacked with metal carding combs he is inextricably associated with injuries to the throat, and is the patron saint of wool-carders. He also became the patron saint of wild animals and died in 361. His saint's day is 3 February.

St Mildred (Whippingham) was a Kentish princess, daughter of Egbert, King of Mercia. Her mother founded a monastery at Thanet in Kent where Mildred became the abbess. She was revered for choosing a religious life over one of plenty.

St Lawrence (St Lawrence) was an early Christian, charged with looking after the church's goods and caring for the poor. In his possession was the Holy Grail, which he sent to his parents for safekeeping in Spain. On the orders of the emperor Valerian, he was martyred by toasting on a gridiron, becoming the patron saint of cooks and chefs. He died in AD 258.

St Edmund (Wootton) was King of the East Angles. Edmund seems to have been martyred around 865, having fought unsuccessfully against the Danes. He was tied to a tree and shot with arrows so that he 'bristled like a hedgehog.'

St Swithin (Thorley) was bishop of Winchester and tutor to the son of King Egbert of Wessex. One miracle is associated with him, the restoration of a basket of eggs belonging to an old lady that had been maliciously broken by workmen. He asked to be buried modestly outside the cathedral but was later moved inside.

His saint's day is 15 July, from which the belief has arisen that 'St Swithin's day if thou dost rain, for forty days it will remain.' Likewise, a dry St Swithin's day forecasts another forty dry days.

St Boniface (Bonchurch) was a Devon man and a missionary in what is now France. He converted the Pagans to Christianity by cutting down a sacred tree dedicated to Thor. When Thor wasn't bothered, the locals accepted the new faith.

Wellow Baptist Church and its Sunday school are both the oldest on the Island.

The Island's first mosque opened in Newport in 2005.

The Bad?

Miss Fanny Oglander, writing to her cousin Henry in India, reported that hayricks valued at £200 had been burned in Newport and Freshwater. Arson was also attempted against Mr Woodrow the builder, who, with Mr Yelf, owned a threshing machine. They had received a letter from 'Swing' saying that everything they had would be destroyed by fire. Yelf abandoned the machine and Woodrow took it to his farm. Captain Swing was a possibly mythical character, figurehead of the agricultural unrest in the 1830s.

Fanny's brother, William, later wrote to Henry that following disturbances by local labourers, ricks had been set alight and seven men transported for life while others got fourteen years.

Thou Shalt not Kill?

The Island's most notorious murder took place in 1736 when Michael Morey, a woodsman living at Sullens, east of Newport, killed his fourteen-year-old grandson, James Dove, severing his head with a billhook. The motive was never established. What is certain is that it was a premeditated murder, for James was killed in a wood and his body mutilated and concealed. Being unable to explain James's absence, Michael ran away but was arrested. About two months later the decomposing body of James was discovered and identified by his clothes. James was buried in Arreton churchyard and Michael was sent to Winchester to stand trial for the murder. He was found guilty and publicly executed, his body being returned to hang in chains at Arreton. The spot, a Bronze Age burial mound, is still known as Michael Morey's Hump. A skull displayed in the nearby Hare and Hounds pub is said to be Michael's.

I Blame the Noncomformists

On 21 June 1812, Elizabeth Hill of Shalfleet, wife of the shoemaker, was hacked to death by her husband's apprentice. The accused, John James, had grown up in the village and at all times had been 'normal'. At the time of the murder, Mr Hill and his son James were away and John declared that had they been at home he would have killed them too.

On being cross-examined, John referred to a biblical text from the book of Job. The judge, Sir Alan Chambre, concluded that James was an 'enthusiastic Methodist' and condemned the dangerous effects of 'vulgar and literal constructions of scriptural passages.' In the face of overwhelming evidence, John was found guilty and hanged, his body handed over for dissection.

Wealth Comes at a Price

Pity poor Mrs Barnaby Leigh of Arreton Manor. Her husband's family acquired the manor following the dissolution of the monasteries, but much good it did them. In 1560, as he lay dying, Leigh's thirteen-year-old son John hurried his father on his way with a pillow over her face. Caught in the act by his young sister Annabelle, he threw her from a window. Mrs Leigh's two brothers, James and Thomas, fought over the inheritance and within three days, both were dead from their wounds.

Foul Deeds

A local feeling of mild regret at the death of Cecil Hambrough on 10 August 1893 changed to avid interest when it was revealed that his tutor, Alfred Motson, had taken out a life insurance on his pupil days before. Hambrough had been mysteriously shot and, believing it to be an accident, his body was returned to the Island for burial. He was laid to rest at St Catherine's Church, Ventnor, his father Dudley being the owner of Steephill Castle.

In December, Dudley witnessed the exhumation of his son. It was revealed that the gunshot came from Motson's weapon and he was put on trial for murder. The day before the shooting, Cecil had been in a boat with Motson that accidentally overturned. Cecil could not swim but managed to hang on to the wreckage until he was rescued. The trial took place in Scotland where the events had occurred and against all the odds the case was found not proven.

For years afterwards, on the anniversary of the 'accident', the Hambroughs put a memorial piece in the *Glasgow Herald* bearing the warning 'Vengeance is mine, I will repay, saith the Lord.'

Thou Shalt Not Steal
September 1852 found William Matthews in court for stealing nectarines from the vicar. As his father undertook to give him 'a good beating,' he was let off with 7/6d costs.

Elizabeth Hunt, a strumpet who stole a pair of boots from Jackman's Shop in the High Street, Ryde, was apprehended in the Fountain Inn, wearing the boots and dancing.

Never Throw Anything Away
When Mrs Lawrence's husband died in Orchard Street, Newport, she failed to report his death. The poor man died of gangrene and his foot was later discovered sitting on a shelf. When charged, Mrs Lawrence said that the offending article had 'fallen off.' The court took no action.

Twelve Good Men and True?
Daniel Boyce unknowingly caused an important change in the law when all attempts to prosecute him for smuggling failed. This was undoubtedly because he always succeeded in bribing both the Sheriff and the jury. In 1733 an Act was introduced stating that the names of jurors must be written down and stored in a box from which they should be drawn at random. Boyce built himself an impressive mansion with sea views called Appley House at Ryde, but after a change in the law he was convicted of smuggling and died in 1740 in the Fleet Prison.

Witchcraft?

Alice Porter, a local girl at Newchurch, was burned as a witch in 1584. Believing that the Devil could gain access to the church from the north, the northern door in All Saints was bricked up.

Molly Downer was a fair-haired, blue eyed and pretty girl who was the illegitimate daughter of the Revd John Barwis, rector of Niton. She and her mother lived in a cottage at Hillway Bembridge, and were generally disapproved of by the good villagers. Molly was believed to consort with smugglers but when her mother died, she became reclusive, existing on a pittance left by her father. Rumours abounded that she was a witch. Molly was said to have cursed a local girl, warning that as she was about to gain good fortune, she would die.

In 1847, on the day that she inherited £20, the girl fell ill, fuelling the villagers' suspicions. Molly died alone and there being nothing of value in the house, the vicar of Bembridge insisted that she should be stripped and searched for any treasure. Nothing was found and she was buried without religious ceremony. In a last act of defiance, Molly left her cottage to her main critic, the same vicar. Highly embarrassed, not to say unnerved, he had the dwelling burnt to the ground.

In July 1888, while out walking, Maud Tomlinson met the new vicar of Yaverland on his way to visit 'poor Mrs Marjoribanks.' He had been coerced into visiting to dispel the rumour that Mrs Marjoribanks had boiled a chicken in the dead of night and the next day the unfortunate cows in the adjacent field had fallen ill. The unhappy lady was in bed with an inflamed leg but no one was willing to go near her.

THREE PRISONS

Parkhurst Juvenile Reformatory, the first of its kind, was opened on the outskirts of Newport in 1838, holding 700 boys plus sixty staff. The boys were expected to remain silent at all times and drilled in moral and religious instruction and useful industrial employment. The purpose was to 'reclaim from infamy' the young criminals.

A first consignment of youngsters was shipped across the Atlantic in 1842 and in 1852, twenty-one boys left for Van Dieman's Land aboard the *Oriental Queen* from Cowes. This led to the first european to be legally executed in Australia. He was John Gavin, a fifteen-year-old Parkhurst boy transported to Western Australia where he murdered George Pollard, the son of his employer. He was publicly executed on 6 April 1844 and buried with no ceremony.

Getaway

In October 1908 Parkhurst's Governor declared that not one escape or attempted escape had taken place in the past year. He added that the conduct of prisoners was satisfactory – considering how weak-minded they were.

Escape from Parkhurst was however a regular event, although most escapees were recaptured within a day. Typical was Henry Hamstead, who took advantage of the fog to abscond but was recaptured a day later at Kitbridge Farm. So hungry was he that he was found raiding the pig bin for food.

Edward Conmey, aged thirty-three, tunnelled his way out of Parkhurst in 1922 and was recaptured twelve days later having carried out a string of burglaries.

Twelve junior offenders achieved a first in 1931 by escaping from Parkhurst and getting to the mainland.

Perhaps the most notorious escape happened in 1995, when three prisoners succeeded in making tools, a ladder, a gun, fake ammunition, a key to all the doors and accumulating £200 in cash before cutting a hole in the outer fence and absconding. They were at large for three days. Following this debacle, Parkhurst Prison was downgraded.

A murderer serving time at Parkhurst sent out details of his planned escape using lemon juice to create invisible ink. This was in 2010. His plan being discovered, he was transferred to another jail.

Deadlier than the Male?

Between 17 April and 8 May 1886, 120 female convicts arrived at Parkhurst mostly from Millbank gaol in London. Angry at the move, they found a focus for their feelings following a visit from Queen Victoria.

The Queen had earlier visited the boys' prison at Parkhurst and had been charmed by the well behaved juveniles to the point of requesting that two of the boys should be released. The women presented an altogether different prospect; turning their backs on Her Majesty and refusing to sing the national anthem. So miffed was she that she

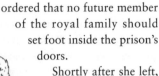

ordered that no future member of the royal family should set foot inside the prison's doors.

Shortly after she left, the women gained access to the yard, ran riot and removed their clothes. The female warders were too scared to approach them so a contingent of male officers was sent for. At first they refused to approach the naked rebels until it was agreed that only the married men should take on the task. Armed with blankets and with the help of a hose, they finally subdued the rioters and returned them to their cells – all in a day's work?

The first steam laundry to be installed in a prison began operation at Parkhurst in 1912.

A Good Thrashing!

Parkhurst was never a hanging gaol but corporal punishment was employed. Following an attack on a warder, a delegation of magistrates ordered the perpetrator to receive six lashes with the cat o'nine tails. This was in 1953.

The last recorded use of the birch was at Camp Hill, an experimental institution opened in 1912 to house habitual criminals. The birching was carried out in 1967, the same year that Albany Gaol was opened to house sex offenders.

All three Island prisons were amalgamated on 1 April 2009.

Famous Prisoners Held on the Isle of Wight

King Charles I spent a year, 1647-8, in Carisbrooke Castle.

William D'Avenant, royalist Poet Laureate, was incarcerated in Cowes Castle in 1650.

Prince Henry of Gloucester and Princess Elizabeth, children of Charles I, arrived at Carisbrooke Castle in 1650. Elizabeth died within weeks and Henry remained for two years before joining his brother, the future King Charles II.

The Kray twins, Reggie and Ronnie, East End gangsters, served time in Parkhurst.

Peter Sutcliffe, dubbed the 'Yorkshire Ripper', was held at Parkhurst.

Peter and Helen Kroger, soviet spies serving their sentence at Parkhurst, were exchanged for British agents in the Soviet Union in 1969.

Freedom of Religion

The fastest growing faith in Albany jail is paganism. In line with prison policy, inmates are allowed to observe two religious festivals a year. Pagans are permitted a robe with no hood, a bendy wand, a pack of tarot cards and an apple to place on the altar – this substitutes for the traditional cider. Practitioners are not permitted to use the cards to tell fortunes.

Traditionally, Jewish prisoners were held at Parkhurst as it provided a synagogue.

Five Star Rating

Following a council survey of 1900 Island kitchens, Albany was given a five star rating, placing it above the Royal Yacht Squadron.

The Dodgy

Perhaps goodness is not all that it seems. A plaque in the porch of Godshill Church to Richard Gard praises his generosity and good deeds, but, according to Sir John Oglander, he was a cheat and rogue. He stole his neighbours' cattle and placed hot loaves on their horns to make them supple so that their shape could be altered.

Why Spelling is Important!

Playwright and priest Nicholas Udall served as vicar of All Saints at Calbourne for three years. He possibly lost his position for religious reasons when catholic Queen Mary I came to the throne. Previously he had been headmaster of Eton College, a 'poorly paid but honourable post,' where he had a reputation as a 'flogger'. During this time he was accused of stealing school plate and also of buggery (a capital offence), for which he was committed to the Marshalsea Prison.

His defenders insisted that the charge was a 'clerical error', and that the word should have been 'burglary!' Whichever, he came under the patronage of Queen Catherine Parr and presented various pageants at court. His lasting drama was a play entitled 'Ralph Roister Doister', recognised as the first English comedy. He died in 1556.

Like a Phoenix in reverse, Jabez Balfour rose to the dizzy heights of financial success before plummeting to earth and spending time in Parkhurst. Jabez, raised in nonconformist piety, founded the Liberator Building Society, intended to enable poor people to buy their own homes. With a flair for making money, he set his eyes on his mother's Island home (she was poor but she was honest), draining and extending areas of Brading Marsh. His financial empire however was built on unstable ground and soon it came toppling down, taking the savings of thousands of people with it, many of whom committed suicide. Jabez fled to Argentina, where he evaded capture for three years but was eventually extradited and sentenced to fourteen years in gaol. Perhaps what people could not forgive was his hypocrisy.

5

(EXTRA)ORDINARY FOLK

THE WEAKER SEX?

In 1784, traveller Henry Wyndham warned women thinking of visiting Freshwater cave, 'it must be observed that this cavern cannot be approached except at low water, and even them, some ladies may find the walk unpleasant for their tender and unsteady feet.'

Girl Power!

No prizes for guessing that Gytha Thorkelsdottir was of Viking descent. She married the Anglo-Saxon nobleman Godwin, Earl of Wessex and her children included King Harold II (he of the arrow) and Gyrth Godwinson, both of whom died at the Battle of Hastings. Their daughter Edith married Edward the Confessor. At the time of Domesday, Gytha was the only woman holding lands on the Island in her own right. Her holdings were at Wroxall and after 1066 they passed to King William. These had been violent times and after the death of King Canute, her husband Godwin is said to have blinded Alfred, son of Ethelred the Unready – how might he have answered when she asked, 'how did you get on at work today, dear?'

Lady Isabella de Fortibus, the richest woman in England, inherited the Island from her brother Baldwin de Redvers when he was poisoned in 1262. Isabella's husband, William de Fortibus, died when she was twenty-three years old and she lived for thirty years at Carisbrooke Castle, avoiding all attempts to marry her off and wrest control of this valuable Island from a woman. The hamlet of Queenbower, near Newchurch, was named for her as she used it as a retreat to watch the hunt. As absolute ruler, from 1280, Isabella claimed all wrecks from the sea around the Island coast. Her children predeceased her and she finally succumbed to royal pressure on her deathbed, selling the Island to King Edward I for 6,000 marks, the equivalent of £4,000. Isabella was the first person in England to use glass for windows.

In 1340, King Edward III's claim to the French throne kept him so busy that he delegated control of the Island to his eldest daughter Isabel, Dame de Coucy, Duchess of Bedford. Isabel, much favoured and pampered, fell in love with Enguerrand VII, Lord of Coucy, a French hostage held at her father's court.

She avoided all other suitors until, in 1385, her father sanctioned their marriage. Showered with gifts, lands and titles, (Isabel became a Lady of the Garter), they lived in France. When Edward was succeeded by King Richard II, de Coucy promptly resigned all his English possessions. Isabel returned to England, where she died in mysterious circumstances. She had two daughters, one spending her life in England and the other in France. The lordship of the Island passed from her to William de Montecute.

When Edward, Duke of York, died at Agincourt in 1415, his wife Phillipa took on the mantle of power as Lady of the Isle of Wight. She died at Carisbrooke on 17 July 1431 and was buried at Westminster Abbey.

Sophie Dawes, one time 'Queen of Chantilly', is the Island's most notorious woman. Born at St Helens in about 1791, the child of Dicky Dawes, a penniless winkle-picker, Sophie was forced into the workhouse, where she was trained for domestic service. Finding her way to London she caught the eye of the elderly Duc de Conde, who amused himself by gentrifying her. He returned to France without giving Sophie a second thought, but she was not to be abandoned that easily. She followed him and installed herself in his household, pretending to be his daughter.

She hoodwinked a member of the royal guard, M. de Feucheres, into marriage so that she could legitimately stay with the Duc. When de Feucheres realised he promptly withdrew from court. Gradually Sophie isolated the ageing Conde, installing her relatives in positions of power and acquiring huge wealth. Having achieved this, the Duc was then found mysteriously hanged, although he was too infirm to have committed suicide. Sophie tried unsuccessfully to take her place in French society but eventually sold her extensive lands and returned to England, buying a house, Bure Homage, at Christchurch in Hampshire.

Her brother James, her one time co-conspirator, mysteriously died on her return to England, fuelling speculation that Sophie had killed him.

He is buried in St Helen's churchyard. Her nephew William used his share of her fortune to purchase the Hermitage near Chale, where he added his own plaque to the Hoy Monument, dominating the landscape. When Sophie died, her estranged husband inherited the bulk of her ill-gotten gains, giving it all to charity.

When Dowsabelle married George Mills, she could not have expected that in 1564 both he and his brother John would die within a year, leaving her a wealthy widow. The brothers George and John had grown rich from the Dissolution of the Monasteries, being paid £1,000 to build Yarmouth Castle. They had already acquired the stone from the destroyed Quarr Abbey and with what was left over constructed the two 'cow' towers at Cowes and upgraded their manor of Hasely Manor at Arreton.

In 1565 a new governor arrived on the Island, Sir Edward Horsey. As a soldier he had served in France, leaving behind his French wife. On meeting Dowsabelle he deserted the official residence at Carisbrooke Castle and moved in with her, scandalising Island society. However, because of their position the locals soon overcame their scruples and the two entertained lavishly, Dowsabelle having the reputation of being the 'best housekeeper in England.'

Horsey died from the plague in 1582. When Dowsabelle died is not recorded but by 1603 the manor belonged to Sir Richard Mills.

Few women were of sterner stuff than Lady Frances Portland, wife of the Island's royalist governor who, in August 1642, was living with her five children at Carisbrooke Castle. When parliamentary forces demanded the castle's surrender, the Countess promptly stepped outside and declared that she personally would light the first cannon to hold them at bay. Eventually an agreement was negotiated and Lady Portland went to France, her children joining their father in England.

Newport Corporation achieved a first in 1931 by voting Mrs Ruby Chandler as the Mayor. Ruby designed the layout of Church Litten burial ground as a park and received the OBE. She was also granted Freedom of the Borough of Newport. She died aged ninety in 1972.

The story of Dorothy Osborne is the epitome of Romeo and Juliet. In 1648 she and her brother visited the Island en route to Guernsey, where their father was royalist governor. At Carisbrooke she met William Temple, cousin of the Parliamentarian governor Robert Hammond, who was responsible for preventing King Charles I from escaping. There was an instant and mutual attraction and William agreed to accompany Dorothy and her brother to St Malo.

When their respective parents discovered, William was banished to the continent and a series of 'suitors' was found for Dorothy, all of whom she avoided. The couple kept up a long and loving correspondence, although only hers survive as she destroyed William's letters for fear of discovery.

Finally in 1654 the parents relented, at which time Dorothy suffered from smallpox and was badly scarred, but the pair married and produced eight children, all of whom predeceased them. Dorothy died in 1695 and is buried in Westminster Abbey.

Disgusted of Ryde?

In 1894 an outraged correspondent wrote to the press:

> One day last week a lady road a bicycle through the streets of our town in a very 'mannish' get up as she wore breeches, and, as far as attire was concerned, looked much like the gentleman bicyclist who accompanied her. Possibly the variety of burlesque artists on the stage are responsible for familiarising us with ladies whose garb is the reverse of flowing... women were, by Mosaic law, sternly forbidden to dress like males, and the public sentiment ought to be against it now.

So there!

Two years later Dr Dabbs, a respected local physician who published a weekly journal, was more approving of cycling for girls. He wrote, 'I say the Psycho is the best ladies' machine for the Wight. The secret is this, that cycles, for ladies, should be a matter of careful measurement, they are infinitely more important as to leg and hip fit than a dress'. However, even he would only go so far. With regard to lady footballers, he commented, 'I have not seen them play: I hope I shall not… and upon my medical word, I do not think a kicking lady is the most graceful kind of lady … but I do like to see a real woman in real skirts'. Really doctor!

Heaven Forbid!

Island MP Sir Barrington Simeon was in no doubt about how far a woman should be let loose. Speaking in the House in February 1897 on votes for women, he warned that there were a million more women than men. Hence, if ever they got the vote they would swamp the males and 'if ever they got into Parliament the end of this country would not be far off.'

The Changing Face of the Island?

Following Lord Tennyson's arrival at Freshwater, young Anne Thackeray, daughter of the novelist William Makepeace, was overheard to ask; 'Is there no one who is commonplace here? Is everybody either a poet, or a genius, or a painter, or peculiar in some way?'

Tennyson was visited by many famous people, among whom were Prince Albert, Robert Browning, Lewis Carol, Charles Darwin, Benjamin Disraeli, Giuseppe Garibaldi, William Gladstone, William Herschel, Charles Kingsley, Edward Lear, Henry Wadsworth Longfellow, John Everett Millais, Ellen Terry and George Frederick Watts. His nearest neighbour was photographer Julia Margaret Cameron. For four days, Queen Emma of Hawaii was also a guest.

When Oscar Wilde visited the Island in October 1884, he had his photograph taken by Messrs Hughes and Mullins, photographers to Queen Victoria at Osborne. Their premises were in Union Street, Ryde, where Wilde was delivering a lecture on dress at the Town Hall. Whilst the reporter for the local *Observer* was charmed by the poet, the journalist from the *Advertiser* condemned Wilde's 'conceited nothings' and 'namby pamby notions.' You can't please everyone!

When the architect John Nash died in 1835, his coffin was taken to St James's Church at East Cowes in the dead of night, to prevent his creditors from stealing his body. Nash, a little man 'pert, impudent and ugly,' designed much of Regent Street and Carlton House Terrace in London and the Royal Pavilion at Brighton. He also converted Buckingham House into a palace for his friend and patron George IV. On the Island he built the Guildhall and the Institute in Newport plus Northwood House at Cowes for his wealthy friends, the Wards. He gave the land, his plans and £100 towards the construction of St James's Church in East Cowes. His home of East Cowes Castle was sold to pay his debts and was demolished in 1960.

In 1881, Henry Knight, an inventor living in the Jubilee Arcade in Ryde, patented a new tin opener. He sold the patent to Cross and Blackwell who made a fortune from it. Knight imported marble statues from Italy, some of which can still be seen on top of No. 64 Union Street, Ryde, next to the arcade. His son Charles had the dubious honour of taking the only photograph of Queen Victoria smiling.

War Heroes

Husband and wife Henry and Mary Gartside-Tipping both appear on Binstead war memorial, having been killed on active service in separate incidents during the First World War. Henry, aged sixty-five, volunteered as lieutenant commander in the mercantile marine reserve, being the oldest serving naval officer. He was killed on 25 September 1915 aboard the yacht *Sanda* off Zeebrugge. Mary, aged forty-seven, took work in a munitions factory but in 1917 volunteered for secret work in France, where she was shot by a deranged French soldier. The French authorities had withdrawn the Croix de Guerre for women but reinstated it especially to honour Mary.

A Victorian feature of Newport was the Olde Curiosity Shoppe in Holyrood Street. Owned by Mr William Ledicott it displayed an array of oddities, not least a bone and a strand of hair belonging to King Charles I's daughter, Princess Elizabeth. After he had owned it for several years, it came to the attention of Queen Victoria, who was less than amused. Mr Ledicott received several visits from detectives and a letter from the Secretary of State telling him to return the precious items to the Princess's grave forthwith. Mr Ledicott did not see how he could return it as the Princess was buried and in any case, he questioned the difference between his own display and museums exhibiting human artefacts. He finally succumbed and sent the offending articles to the governor, Princess Beatrice.

After a career as seismologist in Japan, John 'Earthquake' Milne retired to Shide Hill House just outside Newport with his Japanese wife Toni, where he continued to experiment with earth tremors. Keeping precise records, there was some mystery about a weekly flurry of seismic activity in his laboratory, until it was discovered that two members of his staff had the same afternoon free and met for a passionate interlude in the adjoining room. Milne died in 1913 and is buried in St Paul's Church at Barton. Toni returned to Japan. Two flowering cherry trees were planted in his memory along the River Medina at Shide by the Japanese ambassador.

G.F. Coster JP, a retired diamond merchant, died at Shanklin in 1909. His claim to fame is that he cut the kohinoor diamond.

In March 1894, H.M. Stanley, famous for his meeting with Dr Livingstone, spent a week at Shanklin but refused to entertain the locals with a lecture.

Mr Walters, 'inventor of the paper collar', built a house, the Priory, at Shanklin in 1864.

Queen Elizabeth Slept Here?
No, she didn't, but plenty of famous people have.

In the summer of 1874, Karl Marx came to stay in Ryde with his wife, Jenny. They lodged at No. 11 Nelson Street. After her death, he returned twice to Ventnor, spending the winters of 1881 and 1882 at No. 1 St Boniface Gardens. Marx, the most influential political philosopher of the nineteenth century, suffered permanently from ill health and poverty. The climate of Ventnor fortuitously alleviated his lung condition, but could not cure it. He died in London and is buried at Highgate Cemetery, a mere eleven people attending his funeral. He is one of a select few to have a blue plaque on the house where he stayed at Ventnor.

No pop star could have received a more ecstatic welcome than the Italian freedom fighter Giuseppi Garibaldi. Arriving at Cowes he was met by some 2,000 people, the local paper reporting that he was 'the greatest man ever to set foot on our [Island] soil.' He stayed with his friends Charles and Mary Seely at Brook House and visited Lord Tennyson at Farringford, where, according to Emily Tennyson, people 'waited at our gate for two hours for him.' He received a similar welcome passing through Newport. His visit lasted one week from 4-11 April 1864. Following the Brook visit, a romantic correspondence lasting for ten years developed between Garibaldi and Mary Seely, who snipped off a lock of his hair as a keepsake.

Mohandas Karamchand Gandhi visited the Isle of Wight in 1890 when he was twenty-one years old. He stayed at No. 25 Madiera Road in Ventnor and while he was there his first photograph in England was taken when he visited the Isle of Wight Vegetarian Society.

Haile Selassie was crowned Emperor of Ethiopia in 1930, his line believed to descend from King Solomon. In 1938 he holidayed in Ventnor, where he visited his friend the novelist H. de Vere Stacpoole. Stacpoole lived at Bonchurch and donated the village pond to the community as a bird sanctuary.

With the £5 Edward Elgar earned from composing a piece of music 'Salute d'Amour' for his sweetheart Alice, he was able to afford a honeymoon on the Isle of Wight. Horrified at her choice of bridegroom, Alice's parents disowned her. The couple spent most of their honeymoon at No. 3 Alexandra Gardens, Ventnor, where a blue plaque records their visit.

Havenstreet was fortunate when John Rylands, owner of the UK's largest textile empire and Manchester's first multi-millionaire, bought a retirement home in the village. He donated the Longford Institute to the people, an impressive building with public rooms and a library. Unfortunately the people of Havenstreet seem to have found little use for it and it went through several incarnations before being converted to retirement flats. The King of Italy decorated Rylands for his generosity to the poor of Rome.

Thomas Letts escaped from the stressful life of diaries to find solitude at his house Southview at Blackgang. Here he erected a temple and fountain to celebrate the tercentenary of Shakespeare's birth. The vagaries of nature have since demolished the house, temple and fountain; the road now leads to nowhere.

Almina, widow of Lord Carnarvon of Tutankhamun fame, lived at Eastmore House, Bouldnor in the 1930s. The illegitimate daughter of Lord Alfred de Rothschild, it was her dowry that paid for the Egypt expeditions.

In 1850, Lord Macaulay joined the visitors to Bonchurch. While there he worked on his *History of England*.

Winston Churchill was a sickly child and spent time with his nanny, Mrs Everest, at Ventnor for his health.

ISLAND BORN AND BRED

The Island's most influential son must be Robert Hooke, born at Freshwater in 1630, son of the local curate. A sickly child, Robert became chemical assistant to the anatomist Dr Thomas Willis at Christ Church, Oxford.

Mechanics, astronomy, entomology, architecture, timepieces, springs, light, all occupied his enquiring mind. After the Great Fire of London he was employed as Surveyor of London and with Sir Christopher Wren supervised the re-building of much of the capital. A fellow of the Royal Society and professor of geometry at Gresham College, he published his *Micrographia*, which, according to Pepys, was the most ingenious book he had ever read. Hooke nevertheless felt that his talents had not been recognised, crossing swords with Sir Isaac Newton.

It was with Hooke in mind that Newton made the famous observation that if he had seen further it was through standing on the shoulders of giants. The love of his life seems to have been his niece Grace, who came to live with him at the age of fourteen and with whom he had a questionable relationship. Robert died, blind and seemingly poverty stricken in London, although he left several thousand pounds in a chest. His name is commemorated through Hooke Hill at Freshwater, where the family farmhouse once stood.

Admiral Thomas Hopson, son of a naval captain, was baptised at Shalfleet Church in 1643. Following a distinguished naval career, he was knighted for his part in the Anglo-Dutch wars and became MP for Newtown. He died at Weybridge in 1717. Folklore declares that he was an orphan, apprenticed to a tailor in Niton and one day he disappeared. Assumed to have drowned, in fact he had run away to sea. He returned rich and successful, visiting his old benefactors who did not recognise him.

John Dennett, a Carisbrooke man, had the satisfaction of saving many lives at sea with his rocket-propelled lifesaving equipment that fired a line from the shore to stricken ships. Following the successful rescue of nineteen members of the crew of the *Bainbridge* and the dramatic sinking of the *Irex* in 1890, when twenty-nine crew members were safely winched ashore, the rocket became widely used.

At Gunville, John and his son Horatio ran their own workshop making the equipment and by 1853, 120 coastguard stations had their rockets. John, who described himself as having a fondness for naval and military mechanics, was for many years the custodian of Carisbrooke Castle. He and Horatio are buried in Carisbrooke churchyard.

During the 1840s and 1850s W.M. Norman, a self-educated Island man, was the organiser of the Ventnor Chartists. The first Charter, a petition of 1839 seeking electoral reforms, contained 574 Island signatures and that of 1842, 502 signatures. The 1848 petition does not survive. Ultimately the Chartists ran out of steam but many of their demands were later implemented.

Uffa Fox, the celebrated yacht builder and friend of Prince Philip, bought the old chain ferry that crossed from East to West Cowes to use as a base and workshop, thus avoiding the need to pay local rates. His wife often returned from an outing to find that it had disappeared in her absence. She then had to scour the banks of the Medina to find it.

Apart from designing racing dinghies, Uffa developed an airborne lifeboat, saving the lives of many airmen ditched at sea during the Second World War. Uffa went to the school at Whippingham, designed by Prince Albert, and served a local apprenticeship. His mother was part of Queen Victoria's royal household staff at Osborne.

Anthony Minghella, born at Ryde, became the Island's favourite son. His huge success as a film writer and director produced such gems as *Truly Madly Deeply* and *The English Patient*. He also wrote scripts for iconic TV series such as *Morse*. His glittering career was cut short by his early death. His brother Dominic is also a playwright.

Disappearing Guineas?
When Prince Albert bought Alverstone Farm, not far from Osborne, he apparently paid the owner in guineas. The old man, Mr Cross, retired to Calbourne and was known sometimes to show off his wealth, kept in a bag. When the family went to bed, a ladder giving access to the upper rooms was pulled up and the old man slept with a blunderbuss to guard his savings. When he died his daughter inherited his fortune, but when she died a few years later, there was no sign of the money.

Five Tragic Deaths before their Time

Edward Lewis Miller was on holiday with his parents, exploring the cliffs above Freshwater Bay, when he slipped and fell to his death. His grieving parents erected an obelisk to Edward near the site with the warning: 'thou knowest not what the day may bring forth.' Fifteen-year-old Edward was buried at Goudhurst, Kent.

Francis Gray Bacon was fourteen when he fell from his pony while riding along the Undercliff. His mother, following behind in her carriage, witnessed the accident. Her daughter had recently died in America. Francis, a brilliant child, was buried at Ventnor cemetery and a stone beneath iron railings marks the fatal spot.

Valentine Gray had suffered a life of neglect and violence. In January 1822 his body was found in an outhouse at Scarrots Lane, Newport. He had been beaten to death. Valentine, apprenticed to a chimney sweep, was just ten. He was buried in Church Litten at Newport and a memorial was raised by public subscription. His employers, Mr and Mrs Davis, were imprisoned for manslaughter. He probably inspired the book *The Water Babies* whose author, Charles Kingsley, often visited Lord Tennyson at Freshwater. Outrage at the case resulted in the Climbing Boys' Act, increasing the age at which children could be thus employed. It was fifty years before the practice was prohibited.

Duncan MacDonald, 'Little Don', was only twenty-one-months old when he wandered off with a little friend at Cowes in July 1905 and fell into a lime pit, suffering fatal burns. He was buried at Northwood cemetery, his parents' only child. A statue of a small child marks his grave.

A memorial on the remote beach at Hamstead commemorates the lives of friends David Horace Cox and William Hope Pollack, who drowned when their boat capsized. Eighteen months later, the Cox family lost a second son in a boating accident. The memorial at Hamstead bears the defeated acknowledgement that 'The Sea is His.'

6

THAT'S ENTERTAINMENT

The Devil finds Work?
In Newport, a fine of one shilling was imposed by Puritans on parents who allowed their children to play on a Sunday.

It Pays to Advertise?
In *EastEnders*, Dot Cotton has an Alum Bay sand ornament on her mantelpiece.

King's Mistress Takes to the Boards!
The Theatre Royal at Ryde witnessed one of the last performances by Dorothy Jordan, mistress of King William IV. During their long relationship, Dorothy bore William, then Duke of Clarence, ten children. Their parting came when he unexpectedly became heir to the throne. He quickly put Dorothy aside and sought an acceptable bride. His choice fell on Adelaide, who bore him no surviving children (although she did have a town in Australia named after her). Heartbroken and in poor health, Dorothy retired from the stage in 1816. She then fled to the Continent where she died.

Ellen Terry had her first public performance at the Theatre Royal, playing Puck in *A Midsummer Night's Dream*, while in 1894 thirty freed slaves performed a version of *Uncle Tom's Cabin*. The Theatre Royal lasted until 1961, when a fire destroyed it. From its ashes rose the NatWest Bank.

Royal Command Performance?

Queen Victoria was entertained at Osborne in 1894 by Mr Alfred Loding and his boxing donkey. There being no horse transport, the donkey came by boat as a foot passenger.

American Icons

A statue to Jimi Hendrix stands in the garden of Dimbola Lodge at Freshwater Bay. Nearby, Jimi made his last public recorded performance on Afton Down. The Isle of Wight Rock and Roll Society erected a memorial plaque to Elvis Presley in Rylstone Gardens at Shanklin, despite the fact that he never set foot on the Isle of Wight.

FANCY A PINT?

There were eighty-three licensed premises in Newport in 1903 – and all within walking distance. A hundred years later, just six remain as pubs. They are the Castle (High Street), the Crispin (nearly next door to the Castle), The George (Upper St James Street), The Railway Medina (Sea Street), The Robin Hood (on the site of the old Robin Hood) and The Wheatsheaf (St Thomas's Square).

Fifty-three of these pubs belonged to Island brewers Mew Langton. When the brewery received a warrant to supply beer to Queen Victoria at Osborne, the name Royal was added. Their premises occupied much of central Newport with access to the river Medina so that they could ship hogsheads of wallop to the mainland and beyond.

Mew Langton was the first brewery to introduce a screw top beer can, intended to transport its India Pale Ale – to India. Having been taken over by Whitbread, a mysterious fire removed the listed building, allowing the area to be developed.

In 1735 Yarmouth boasted six pubs – the Bugle, the King's Head, the Wheatsheaf, the Bull's Head, the Whyte Lion and the New Inn. Only the first three remain.

Carisbrooke once had seven pubs – the Waverly, the Cutter's Arms, the George, the Bugle, the Red Lion, the Eight Bells and the Castle Hotel. The Eight Bells and the Waverly have survived.

Niton offered five drinking establishments – the Goose, the Star, the Cat and Rabbit, the White Lion and the Buddle. Only the last two remain.

The Colwell Bay Inn at Colwell was previously named the Nelson in honour of the naval hero. Before that it had been known as the Drum and Monkey.

In 1870, the Blacksmith's Arms above Carisbrooke was run by local blacksmith George Arnold. Previously it was called Ye Old Betty's Aunt. George shod ponies for Queen Victoria at the Osborne Estate.

Bill of Fayre

The Buddle Inn at Niton could offer you an 'egg flip', consisting of a quart of beer, twelve eggs and half a pint of brandy warmed over the fire, or, on a warm day, a 'dog's nose', an egg flip minus the eggs and served cold.

Newtown had its pub – the Newtown Arms – generally known as Noah's Ark. It closed in 1916.

Newbridge had the Horse and Jockey, while Wellow had the Sun.

Joseph and Matthew Phripp were accused of running an unlicensed alehouse in Cowes and failing to pay Hearth Tax on an empty property in 1671.

Fancy a Little Something?

Touring in 1797, Henry Wyndham noted a vineyard planted at Sea Cottage, along the Undercliff. Occupying an acre of land, a French vigneron was imported to oversee it. Wyndham predicted that:

> if a scorching climate alone is sufficient to ensure its success, there
> can be no doubt of it; but whether the spray of the neighbouring

sea, may not blast the foliage of the vines, or whether the land may not be too moist and spongy... a few years' experience will ultimately determine.

Within five years, the vineyard had failed. It quickly became a tourist attraction and he pointed out that, 'The novelty of the vineyard has probably attracted more company to St Lawrence than the picturesque, romantic scenery.'

Drinking wine on the Island isn't new. The vineyard at Adgestone is reputed to be the oldest in the county, standing on the site of that planted by the Romans. Other Island vineyards are the Rosemary near Ryde and Rossiters at Wellow.

Anyone for the Skylark?
Wyndham, a self-appointed expert on tourism, advised that a trip around the coast would take between fourteen and twenty-four hours, depending on the wind and tides. He warned that seasickness and anxiety in rough weather was likely and that 'ladies and gentlemen only, who possess an uncommon degree of cheerfulness [*sic*] and good humour and are proof against the convulsive operations of a sea-sickness' should risk it.

Island's Oldest Tourist Attractions
In 1648, King Charles rode to Alum Bay to view the Needles (then with its original 100ft-tall needle), before stopping to dine with the Urrys at Thorley.

In 1817, John Keats made a point of visiting Carisbrooke Castle and Shanklin Chine.

Blackgang Chine opened to the public in 1843. Still operating today, they claim to be the oldest theme park in the country.

Winkle Street at Calbourne (official name Barrington Row) is a picture postcard row of cottages complete with sheepwash. Hard to believe that it was once described as tumbledown, housing farm workers, piggeries and the slaughterhouse. The sheepwash was still in use in the 1970s.

The Pen and the Sword?

Writers Robert Graves and A.A. Milne were patients at Osborne Convalescent Home during the First World War.

FILMS AND TELEVISON SERIES FILMED ON THE ISLE OF WIGHT

Man in a Suitcase (1967) – Mystery with Cowes seafront doubling as Corfu Docks.

Endless Night (1971) – Based on an Agatha Christie novel partly shot on Mottistone Down.

Something to Hide (1972) – Nicholas Montserrat thriller filmed around Bembridge.

That'll be the Day (1973) – 1950s Rock n' Roll adventure starring David Essex and Ringo Starr.

Julia (1977) – Twentieth Century Fox bio-drama with some Island scenes.

Return of the Saint (1978) – double episode 'The Saint and the Brave Goose', includes Cowes powerboat races.

The Wildcats of St Trinians (1980) – has Island scenes.

The Trespasser (1981) – D.H. Lawrence novel starring Alan Bates and set in Freshwater.

Inspector Wexford Series (1987-2000) – Ruth Rendall mysteries, partially filmed on the Isle of Wight.

Lady Chatterley's Lover (1993) – Based on D.H. Lawrence's novel. Director Ken Russell, starring Joely Richardson and Sean Bean, filmed at Bonchurch, Black Gang and St Lawrence.

Mrs Brown (1997) – Directed by John Madden. It depicts the relationship between Queen Victoria and John Brown, starring Dame Judi Dench and Billy Connolly. Partly filmed at Osborne House.

The English Patient (1997) – Directed by Anthony Minghella. Includes some Isle of Wight footage.

The Winslow Boy (1999) – Directed by David Mamet from the play by Terence Ratigan. Starring Nigel Hawthorne and Jeremy Northam; it is based on an incident at the Royal Naval College, Osborne. It was shot at Osborne House.

Hotel Paradiso (1999) – Director Adrian Edmondson. Starring Rik Mayall and Simon Pegg. Chaotic comedy.

Reach for the Moon (2000) – TV series set in a school. Starred Peter McInery and Linda Bellingham. Filmed at Carisbrooke High School

New Year's Day (2001) – Youth drama by local director Suri Krishnamma.

Message to Love (2002) – Director Murray Lerner. Film footage of the 1970 Pop Festival at Afton Down, featuring Jimi Hendrix's last filmed performance.

Amnesia (2004) – Psychological drama starring John Hannah.

Fragile (2005) – Psychological drama starring Calista Flockhart.

Speed of Light (2007) – Science fiction thriller.

Some Novels Set on the Isle of Wight

England, England – Julian Barnes – (futuristic: The Isle of Wight as a Theme Park).

Mary of Carisbrooke – Margaret Campbell Barnes – (Royalist adventures of King Charles at Carisbrooke Castle).

Coppins Bridge series – Elizabeth Daish – (family sagas in Newport).

The Trespasser – D.H. Lawrence – (an illicit weekend in Freshwater).

Day of the Triffids – John Wyndham – (science fiction), ends on the Island.

Undercliff Trilogy Wendy – K. Harris – (contemporary lives set south of Ventnor).

The Silence of Dean Maitland – Maxwell Gray (Mary Gleed Tuttiett) – (gothic romance set in the village of 'Malbourne').

Moonfleet – John Mead Faulkner – (eighteenth-century adventure ending at Carsbrooke Castle).

Writers Born on the Isle of Wight

Ray Allen, born and resident in Ryde, wrote the first script of *Some Mothers do 'Ave Em* when working as a cleaner at the Regal Cinema, Shanklin.

Adrian Searle, art critic for the *Guardian* newspaper, writes widely about Isle of Wight history.

Elizabeth Missing Sewell, 'Authoress, Novelist and Pioneer', was born in Newport. When her minister father died penniless, she took on responsibility for his debts, financed by her morally uplifting books for girls. She made it be known that 'boys are sent into the world to govern…girls to dwell in quiet homes.' She died at Bonchurch in 1906 at the age of ninety-one, maintaining the view that 'a woman who is not feminine is a monster in creation.'

Patricia Sibley, who was born on the Island, was a successful novelist and non-fiction writer. She died on the Island in 2004 aged seventy-six.

Philip Norman's book *The Skaters' Waltz* recounts a dysfunctional childhood in Ryde.

Janet Mary Tomson, born in Shanklin, has written Elizabethan, Victorian, Civil War and contemporary novels set on the Island.

Contemporary novelist Patrick Gale was born here.

Locally-born Carol Barton has produced at least forty novels for publishers Mills and Boon.

Writers Writing on the Isle of Wight

Both Charles Darwin and Charles Dickens stayed at the Norfolk House Hotel in Shanklin. Whilst there, Dickens started to write *David Copperfield*, later moving to Bonchurch.

Christopher Isherwood is remembered for *Mr Norris Changes Trains*, on which the musical Cabaret is based, visited the West Wight in the 1930s.

John Oliver Hobbs (real name Pearl Craigie) lived at St Lawrence. She was a daughter of American industrialist John Morgan Richards, who owned Steephill Castle. She was a highly successful novelist and was tipped to write the official biography of Benjamin Disraeli. A friend of Lord Conroy, viceroy of India, she died tragically young in her thirties. Her house, Craigie Lodge at St Lawrence, bears a plaque in her memory.

J.B. Priestly came in 1933, living first at Billingham Manor then at Brooke House. He entitled his biography *Rain over Godshill*. His best remembered work from this time is *An Inspector Calls*, written in 1947.

Aubrey de Selincourt, teacher and headmaster, retired here in 1947, devoting himself to writing. He lived at Nutkins at Niton with his poet wife Irene Rutherford McCloud. His family owned the Swan and Edgar store at Piccadilly. Their daughter Lesley married Christopher Robin Milne of *Winnie the Pooh* fame. De Selincourt died in 1962.

Lewis Carroll author, of *Alice in Wonderland,* visited the Tennysons and the Camerons in 1859. Like Julia Margaret Cameron, Carroll had taken up photography.

William Adams, clergyman, came to Bonchurch when in ill health. His allegorical work *The Shadow of the Cross* was a favourite of William Wordsworth. Adams is buried in Bonchurch old church.

Frances Barclay, Victorian novelist, is buried at St Peter's Church, Seaview.

Edward Thomas, poet and writer, wrote *The Isle of Wight.* Thomas died at Arras in 1917.

After visiting her great aunt, the photographer Julia Margaret Cameron, Virginia Woolf wrote a tongue-in-cheek play *Freshwater.*

Contemporary Writers
Brian Hinton, poet and writer, lives at Totland. He wrote the definitive account of the 1970 Pop Festival: Message to Love.

Mei Trow, Ryde teacher, writes both fiction and non-fiction on a variety of subjects.

Diana Kimpton is a highly-successful writer of children's books, both fiction and non-fiction.

Poets Writing on the Isle of Wight
John Keats visited in 1817 and 1819 and wrote what is now Shanklin's motto 'A Thing of Beauty is a Joy Forever.' (Actually written on Bowcombe Down.)

Algernon Swinburne, 'a fragile little creature', was the only one of his siblings not born on the Island but he stayed when they left. The family home was at East Dene in Bonchurch and Algernon later stayed at Northcourt in Shorwell. His father, an Admiral, 'taught' poor Algernon to swim by flinging him head first into the sea. He is buried at Bonchurch.

Thomas Hardy visited Swinburne's burial place, writing an elegy over the grave entitled *A Singer Asleep*. John Betjeman wrote of Swinburne, 'No one made the sea hiss and clang in English poetry better than he.'

Alfred Lord Tennyson turned sleepy Freshwater into a place of pilgrimage when he moved there. Among his voluminous output was the 'Charge of the Light Brigade', written on Tennyson Down, 'Crossing the Bar' while sailing across to the Island, 'Enoch Arden', which was composed in his little shed in the garden, and 'Come into the Garden Maud' which became a popular Victorian song.

Sir William Davenant, Poet Laureate and godson of William Shakespeare, shared the fate of his monarch Charles I, being imprisoned on the Island.

Gerard Manly Hopkins spent a summer with his family at Shanklin Manor, extolling the beauties of the locality. His brother Arthur, a gifted painter, later worked for the *Graphic* and *Punch* magazines. Gerard himself illustrated his letters of the time with line drawings.

Alfred Noyes, immortalised by his poem 'The Highwayman', took up residence along the Undercliff.

Rudyard Kipling's father Lockwood trained the young artist Bai Ram Singh, who created the decoration of the Durbar Room at Osborne. When the original Osborne House was being demolished, Rudyard acquired some leather wall coverings that he described as 'lovelier than our wildest dreams,' installing them at his home at Batemans. His poem 'A Centurian's Song' features a hero having 'Served in Britain forty years from Vectis to the Wall,' feeling more at home in Britain than Rome, a feeling no doubt shared by many Romans after nearly 400 years of occupation.

John Sterling was so admired by Thomas Carlisle, that the great man wrote his biography. Sterling suffered from the nineteenth-century scourge of tuberculosis and fled to the Island following the death of his wife in childbirth. He bought a house, Hillside, at Ventnor but had little time to enjoy it. He is buried in Bonchurch old churchyard.

W.H. Auden was a frequent visitor to the West Wight ,while acclaimed writer Edward Upward lived at Sandown.

David Gascoigne, surrealist poet, spent his final years at Northwood. He met his wife Judy when she visited Whitecroft hospital to read poetry where David was a patient, unknowingly selecting one of his verses. He died on the Island in 2001 aged eighty-five.

Louis Macniece, poet, novelist and playwright, owned a holiday home on the Island.

Perhaps John Gwilliam (1790-1845) suffered from 'rhymer's disease' – recording everything in verse. His prolific output included two volumes extolling the Isle of Wight – *Rambles in the Isle of Wight 1841-2*; and *Norris Castle: a recent tramp in the Isle of Wight 1845.*

Edmund Peel, cousin of Prime Minister Robert Peel, also suffered from a surfeit of words. After a military career, Edmund lived with his brother at Under Rock in Bonchurch. The *Gentleman* magazine regarded his 483-page eulogy of the Island, *The Fairest Isle,* as only skin deep.

Regarding Bonchurch, Edmund wrote, 'Come, look on Bonchurch from the sacred steep, Whose springs salubrious gush with life and light …' The reader may judge its merits. Edmund died locally.

Visiting Shanklin in 1868, Henry Longfellow was so inspired by the Chine that he wrote a verse for the occasion: 'Oh Traveller stay thy weary feet, Drink of this fountain pure and sweet, It flows for rich and poor the same. Then go thy way remembering still, the wayside well beneath the hill, the cup of water in his name.' The verse is inscribed above the drinking fountain at the top of Chine Hill. Longfellow stayed at the Holliers Hotel.

Artists Painting on the Isle of Wight

George Morland, landscape painter, chose the Island as a refuge to escape his creditors. (*See* chapter 2, Smuggling).

One has the impression that Thomas Rowlandson's tour of the Island passed in a haze of alcohol. Along with his brother-in-law Samuel Howett, he paid two rollicking visits in 1784 and 1791 recording the scenery as they went.

Joseph Mallord William Turner visited several times, staying with his friend John Nash at East Cowes Castle, during which time he sketched prolifically.

Thomas Sidney 'Cow' Cooper's landscape of Carisbrooke Castle, displayed in Osborne House, features his trademark cattle.

Helen Allingham, indelibly associated with rustic cottage scenes, frequently visited with her husband Henry. Henry refused to allow his passion for nude bathing to be interrupted by the arrival of ladies on the beach.

Barbara Boudichon, a talented painter whose mother Ann Longden is buried at Wootton, was a gifted painter. Among her work is a landscape 'At Ventnor', dated 1856. Barbara was a founder of Girton College Cambridge and campaigner for women's suffrage.

Walter Spindler owed his lifestyle to his successful father William, a German chemist who purchased The Old Park at St Lawrence. Energetic and enterprising, Spindler senior planned to construct a seaside resort to rival Ventnor but the power of the sea interfered with his work. Walter seems to have lacked his father's drive but he worked as a painter, his most famous model being Sarah Bernhardt.

Locally acclaimed artist Cavendish Morton recently passed his centenary at Bembridge.

POP FESTIVAL

In 1970, the biggest pop festival ever to take place in the UK was held on Afton Down at Freshwater. It lasted for five days. Feelings ran high, with the Island MP Mark Woodnutt declaring that 'the health of everyone in the Isle of Wight will be endangered.' Six-hundred thousand festival-goers colonised the Island. They were rewarded with fine weather and performances from Joan Baez, Joni Mitchell, The Doors, The Moody Blues, The Who, Free, Kris Kristofferson, Emerson Lake and Palmer, Leonard Cohen, Miles Davis and of course Jimi Hendrix. It was his last public performance captured on film before his death two weeks later. After the festival an Act of Parliament, the Isle of Wight Act, banned such a large gathering happening on the island again. Since 2002, however, regular festivals with limited numbers have taken place.

ENTERTAINERS BORN ON THE ISLAND

Actors – Sheila Hancock, Jack Douglas, Jeremy Irons, Brian Murphy and Marius Goring.

Musicians – Craig Douglas (aka Terry Perkins, local milkman who had twelve hit singles and sold 5 million records), Mark King (singer with Level 42).

Other – Anthony Minghella (film director), Phil Jupitus (comedian), Bear Grylls (adventurer).

Tom Walls, 1920s actor and film producer, owned a house, Fairy Court, at Shanklin. A horseracing enthusiast, he bred the 1932 Derby winner 'April 5th'. The horse was injured in the St Leger and retired from racing, outliving his owner by five years.

The Island's 'Best' Tourist Attractions?
Carisbrooke Castle, a Norman motte and bailey castle, was for many years the centre of Island power. Famous visitors include John Keats, William Wordsworth, Ezra Pound, Andrew Motion, the Queen, Prince Philip, Princess Margaret, Lord Louis Mountbatten, Prince Charles and of course Princess Beatrice, who lived there as Island Governor. Not forgetting King Charles I, who lived there under protest!

Osborne House is an opulent, Italian-style-villa built by newlyweds Victoria and Albert, having knocked down a nice Georgian house in the process. It was visited by Disraeli, Gladstone, Marconi, Edward Lear (who taught Queen Victoria how to paint), John Brown (indispensable lackey), and half the Royals of Europe from Kaiser Wilhelm to Czar Nicholas. King Edward VII disliked it so much he gave it 'to the nation.'

Bembridge Windmill is the only windmill remaining on the Island.

Shanklin Chine is a beautiful, natural ravine in the Old Village, extolled by John Keats on his visit in 1817.

Yarmouth's Best Tourist Attraction?
In 1934, the Isle of Wight Council took charge of Yarmouth Bridge and on 16 April 1935 the Island's first traffic lights were installed. The red light proved hazardous to shipping and had to be fitted with a grill but once they were running smoothly, all was peace and light. Their real value however was in being the Island's latest and most novel tourist attraction. Until the 1950s, Round the Island coach tours took visitors to Yarmouth especially to view them.

Island Myths and Legends

Mordred, kinsman and alleged murderer of the saintly King Arthur, was apparently despatched to Carisbrooke Castle, where he was boiled in oil.

All Saint's Church, Godshill, began on an acre of land belonging to a local farmer. Miffed at losing a valuable asset he suggested that being a sinner, this was not the best place to build a church but the Bishop promptly absolved him of all sin, thus solving the problem. Work began but overnight the foundations mysteriously moved to the top of a nearby hill. The farmer was suspected of subterfuge. The stones were returned and a watch kept and to the guard's amazement, the stones moved of their own volition and were next morning found at the top of the hill. Facing the inevitable, the church was built on the top of God's Hill.

Knighton Gorges was described as the most beautiful house on the Island, but it seemed doomed to tragedy. Trouble started with Hugh de Morville, one of the knights who murdered Thomas Beckett. Subsequent owners suffered early death and tragedy, culminating with George Maurice Bisset, who reputedly ran a mini hellfire club attended by both John Wilkes and David Garrick. He became involved in a scandal with Seymour Fleming, provocative wife of local aristocrat Sir Richard Worsley with whom he blatantly spent the night. A salacious court case saw Worsley, humiliated and Bisset being shunned. When his daughter married a clergyman, Bisset had the house demolished to prevent her from inheriting it. He died alone in 1821 in the gardener's cottage.

According to legend, at the back of Farringford House is a wood and beyond that 'Maiden's Croft', which was once part of a Cistercian priory where an 'ever vigilant dragon' guards the mouth of a subterranean way to France.

Queen Eleanor of Acquitaine was supposedly imprisoned and died on the Isle of Wight, being buried at Quarr in a gold coffin.

Isabella de Fortibus, the Lady of the Wight, is rumoured to have had a palace at Middleton, on the outskirts of Freshwater.

A story echoing the Pied Piper of Hamelin, tells how Newtown was overrun by rats. In desperation the residents agreed to pay a piper to rid the town of the pests. As he played the rats came to listen, following him down the streets to the water's edge. There he took a boat and rowed out to sea. The rats followed and one by one were drowned.

When the piper returned for his money the residents decided there was no longer any need to pay him. In revenge, he played another tune that attracted the town's children. As with the rats, he took them to the water and they too perished. This apocryphal tale allegedly accounts for the town's decline.

Bloodstone copse is said to take its name from the blood spilled when marauding Danes and Saxons crossed swords a thousand years ago. The more likely explanation for the name is that the water in the stream is tinged red by algae. Bloodstone and Eaglehead copses are sites of special scientific interest close to Ashey and a burial place for prehistoric peoples.

The Beautiful Game

At a meeting at Warburton's Hotel on 24 November 1877 it was resolved to set up Newport Football Club. A motion that a half-day's holiday for young male shop and office workers be instituted was thrown out. When did the lads find time to play?

Tick Tock

William Hosking of Ventnor made it his business to install a clock at every railway station on the Island.

The sadly silent church clock at All Saints, Freshwater, no longer rings out the Tennyson Chimes, introduced in 1895. The new clock, supplied by Smith of Derby, came with the current equivalent of 'ring tones', and following the recommendation of the vicar's friend, John Stainer, professor of music at Oxford, an amended chime was introduced. If anyone wishes to hear it, they will need to go to the Carfax Tower at Oxford where it is still in use.

Henry Charles Millett, churchwarden at St John's, Wroxall, presented a clock to the church, however, a public subscription had to be set up to raise a tower to accommodate it.

7

ALL CREATURES GREAT AND SMALL

Happy Birthday

The Island's earliest inhabitants are 125 million years old. Twenty-nine different types of dinosaur frequently pop up along our cliffs and beaches, making this one of the richest sources of finds in Europe. The biggest were brachiosaurs – up to 25m long and 7m high. Iguanodons were the most common, once grazing in herds. Dinosaur footprints can still be seen on the beach at Hanover Point. The south coast justifiably gives the Island the name Dinosaur Island, being littered with fossils.

The Farmyard

The Island once had its own breed of pig. In 1802 it was described as tall and large, with black spots and having deep sides. It made excellent bacon – no doubt accounting for its disappearance.

At the beginning of the nineteenth century, 40,000 sheep were shorn every year on the Island. During the winter months many were shipped over to benefit from the milder climate. The names of Lambs Lease and Ramsdown bear witness to past activities.

The affluent Romans had a varied diet. Thanks to them the Islanders got a first glimpse of guinea fowl, peacocks and pheasants, and possibly Spanish rabbits, too delicate to survive an Island winter in the wild. It was 800 years before the ubiquitous bunny really appeared.

The British had their own breed of cattle but the Romans went one better, importing a white variety.

The Romans were partial to oysters, also to a large 'edible' dormouse. Snails were a particular delicacy, fattened on wheat and milk until they could no longer squeeze back into their shells – then fried – how mean is that! A real treat was a whole boar, stuffed with live birds that flew out as the roast was carved. Happy eating!

Q for Queeny

At the first Isle of Wight Agricultural Show in 1882 exhibitors were listed in alphabetical order. The only entry under Q was Her Majesty the Queen. Victoria got into the spirit of things, entering animals in five classes and giving organisers the chance to add the name Royal to the new show. This is how the Queen fared:

Class 3: An Agricultural
Mare with a Foal at Side – HM entered Smart, aged 7 years and was 'Commended.'
Class 15: A Cow in Milk or Calf. QV entered two animals, Gypsy aged 8 and Rose aged 7 who was in milk – Rose was awarded 2nd prize.
Class 16: a Heifer under 3 years – Queen Victoria's unnamed heifer aged 18 months was 'Commended.'
Class 31: A Pen of Ten Chid Sheep – HM was the only entrant and as a result got first prize.

The prize money consisted of either £2 or £3 for first and £1.10/- or £1 for second. I wonder how she spent the money? It is interesting to imagine her wearing a tweed cap, Barbour jacket and wellies but I doubt that she personally trotted around the arena with her exhibits.

Prince Albert the Farmer

When at Osborne, Prince Albert enjoyed the role of farmer on his properties of Barton and Alverstone. Here he kept about forty horses, including eight Clydesdale brood mares and a stallion. Three or four foals were born yearly.

At Barton Manor the prince had about a dozen Alderney cows and a bull. The Alderney was once a familiar sight on the Island but alas the breed no longer exists, the last having been evacuated from Alderney in wartime. There are herds of Guernsey and Jersey cows locally, the latter being closely related to the Alderney. They can rightly claim royal heritage – their ancestor being a bull belonging to Queen Victoria.

Prince Albert made a yearly purchase of about forty Galloways to be fattened. He also had between forty-100 Dorset ewes served by a black-faced ram and a flock of 300 Southdown ewes. His eight breeding sows were of the black Sussex variety.

The prince enthusiastically showed his livestock at Smithfield and would no doubt have entered into the Island show with equal alacrity had he not died.

Sacred Cows

Queen Victoria was squeamish about babyhood and disapproved of her daughter Alice's decision to breastfeed her babies, promptly calling a dairy cow at Barton Farm Alice, after her daughter.

Following the Crimean War, Victoria was introduced to a cow that had supplied milk to the British Headquarters. With scant regard for its feelings, Her Majesty observed that it was a strange looking creature, half-Hungarian with a Roman look.

A lady sunbathing at Compton beach decided to cool off in the sea. She had hardly stood up when a cow, grazing on the clifftop above, came flying down to land on the spot she had just vacated. She was lucky not to be crushed beneath it – the cow was not so lucky, dying from the impact.

Undercliff Jasmine however, a posh cow, fell 60ft to land on St Lawrence beach and was rescued by helicopter. Her owner announced that she had not hurt herself.

A herd grazing on Culver Cliff stampeded when startled by the sudden appearance of the Red Devils' air display. They damaged several cars and scattered picnickers, but fortunately no one was hurt.

Rabbits!

The Normans introduced the rabbit to the Isle of Wight. Mentioned for the first time was a warren at Bowcombe in 1225, when 200 rabbit skins were sold. The flesh of an adult rabbit, known as a cony, was more expensive than poultry. When drawing up land leases the availability of rabbits was always mentioned. The regular trade in rabbits was such that long before a postal service, it was the cony man who came weekly and took back letters and rabbits to the mainland.

In 1303, because of continuous unrest, Thorley estate asked to be excused from paying revenue on its rabbits – because the soldiers had eaten them!

In June 1940 the first victim of a German bomb attack was at Blackgang on the golf course, where a solitary rabbit was nibbling at the turf.

Dead Dogs

Queen Victoria hated cats but was always surrounded by dogs. She particularly favoured collies and the most adored was Noble. Noble and Sharp were sculpted in marble by the Queen's gifted daughter, Princess Louise, and are displayed in the Marble Corridor at Osborne House. In the gardens of Osborne a small plaque marks the burial of Bleny, a pug beloved of Queen Victoria's daughter, Beatrice. The statue of another pug, Bosco, sits outside Queen Victoria's bedroom.

One of the Queen's collies, Morair, has a modest headstone in the grounds of Barton Manor. The Queen made no secret of those she favoured. On Morair's grave she records that he was the 'Son of Noble 2, grandson of Noble, the Queen's favourite for ten years.'

Eos was a dog beloved of Prince Albert, a black greyhound with white feet and a white streak on her nose. She was born in January 1834 when Prince Albert was a lonely, mixed-up teenager. Eos accompanied Queen Victoria and Prince Albert on their first visit to Scotland in 1842, along with the Queen's 'Scotch' Terrier Cairnach (1839-1844). The pets travelled in one of the escorting ships, *Lightning*.

In 1842, Eos was accidentally shot by Queen Victoria's Uncle Ferdinand of Saxe-Coburg. At the time he was attending the christening of the new baby, Albert Edward, the future Edward VII. Ferdinand was General of the Cavalry in the Austrian Army. Happily Eos recovered, although her progress was slow. Having told Queen Victoria's Uncle Leopold about the accident, he replied that it would have been better if Ferdinand had shot some other member of the family.

Eos was painted by Sir Edwin Landseer. When she died, aged ten-and-a-half, Lord Melbourne declared himself to be 'in despair' at the news. She was buried at Windsor, where a bronze statue was erected. Her statue also stands in the grounds of Osborne House, modelled by Prince Albert and cast by John Francis in 1845. In 1974 she was suffering from 'corrosion of the legs', and the Morris Singer Foundry at Basingstoke carried out repairs.

Alfred Lord Tennyson was frequently seen walking on the High Down with 'the beautiful Siberian Wolfhound Karenina', a granddaughter of one that belonged to the late Czar of Russia.' Tennyson also owned an Afghan sheepdog.

At Carisbrooke Castle, Whitgar, a St Bernard dog belonging to the then curator Captain James Markland, lays buried along the motte, his resting place marked by a stone.

The Island could be a dangerous place for dogs. Vanguard, owned by the Chichester family of seafaring fame, mysteriously met his end at Cowes in 1868. Did he perhaps drown? His tomb is in the grounds of Arlington Court, the family home in Devon.

Smut met his end under a train at Wroxall Station to the horror of Lady Florence Dixie, who had been holidaying at Bonchurch. Lady Dixie erected an elaborate monument to him in her married home at

Market Bosworth in Leicestershire. A long poem included the words 'here lies a friend never forgotten.'

Sporran had an unfortunate meeting in 1929 with a motor car in Bonchurch and is buried at the Lake Hotel in Bonchurch.

The Pets at Rest Cemetery, just outside of Newport, provides a satisfying resting place for deceased animal friends where headstones, floral tributes and a chapel of rest bring solace to the mourner.

Blood Sports
In the sixteenth century, Sir John Oglander recorded that the governor, Sir Edward Horsey, stocked the Island with hares, there being not one on the Island.

At Brading the Island's governor was expected to donate five guineas for the purchase of a bull to be baited. The mayor and corporation then watched the gruesome spectacle dressed in full regalia. A dog, known as the Mayor's Dog, was the first to attack the bull, which was tethered to the ring in the town square. The meat was then distributed to the poor.

Killing a bull without baiting it was illegal and in 1592 William Smith was fined 6*d*. Thankfully the custom was finally outlawed and in 1815 George Bead of Cowes was prosecuted at Hampshire Quarter Sessions for bull baiting. Brading bullring was moved from the centre of the road and placed outside the new Town Hall.

In centuries past the Island had extensive woodland given over to hunting. Foxes were brought to the Island about 1845, specifically to be hunted.

From Elizabethan times there were seven deer parks and at the beginning of the nineteenth century, two remained. A deerhound called Watch is said to have killed the last deer in Parkhurst Forest.

Betty Haunt Lane, west of Carisbrooke, has nothing to do with ghosts. A haunt was a place where deer congregated to shelter.

Badgers were not introduced into the Island until the 1920s.

Horse Power

Lord Mottistone was so enamoured of his horse that he wrote the animal's biography, *My Horse Warrior,* and published an obituary on his death. Warrior was foaled at Yafford in 1908 and during the First World War was present at the battles of the Marne, Ypres, the Somme and Cambrai. The *Daily Telegraph* dubbed him the horse the Germans could not kill. A smallish brown gelding, he was trained as a cavalry horse and after the war took part in many victory parades. Warrior was retired to Mottistone, living until 1941. His life ended when war shortages meant that there was no longer sufficient grain to feed him.

Another horse immortalised in print was Frantic, 'my loveable chestnut mare who brought such joy into my life for a quarter of a century.' She belonged to the boat designer and friend of Prince Phillip, Uffa Fox.

He regularly rode from his home at Puckaster Cove, near Niton, to visit a friend at Arreton Manor. The ride took him from the Undercliff to Whitwell, Nettlecombe and over the Down toward Stenbury, then through Godshill Park, Great Budbridge and Perriton. Arriving at Arreton he stayed to dinner and, after copious amounts of alcohol, rode home at around 2 a.m., leaving Frantic to find the way. Below him he could feel the 'warm glow and courage of Frantic coming through the saddle, and I could also feel the glow in her heart stealing through, up into my own.'

The main Newport to Ryde road passes along the 'Racecourse' near the East Cowes turn off. The Queen's estate extended this far and prior to her ownership, annual race meetings were held in this area.

The *Isle of Wight Advertiser* for 13 April 1878 was pleased to report that a fund had been set up to buy a new horse for Mr Joseph Reid, a respectable man whose previous horse had dropped dead in the street. Without it he could not carry out his trade.

In 1828 a horse at Hamstead Farm, belonging to the architect John Nash, was poisoned. The blame was laid at the feet of two labourers dismissed from his service, but there being insufficient evidence one was released and the second held for further questioning. Nash introduced Suffolk Punch horses to his farm.

Horses are not as predictable as machines. Richard Urry had both legs broken in March 1835 as he stepped down from his father's cart and was violently kicked by the mare he was driving. On a happier note, on 23 June 1838 the *Hampshire Telegraph* published the following notice: 'We are happy to state that Mr James Wheeler of Wellow, who was seriously injured by the kick of a horse, and reported to be dead, is now in a fair way of recovery.'

A piebald horse named Jake recently took a walk from his field and, stepping on some unfamiliar ground, found himself shoulder deep in a swimming pool. Happily, the fire brigade was able to get him out unharmed.

In a darker vein, on 4 April 1772 a man named Froyle was taken from the workhouse and buried at Chale. His internment was accompanied by the terse comment 'crippled by a horse that he had used inhumanly.' Serves him right!

Next to the war memorial at Lake stands a drinking trough with a unique dedication: TO THE HORSES AND DOGS WHO ALSO BORE THE BURDEN AND HEAT OF THE DAY 1914-1920.

Carisbrooke Castle is famous for its donkeys, used to draw water from the well by means of a treadmill. Early mentions state that in 1771, after having worked for forty-five years, a donkey died. Another died in 1798 aged thirty-two years.

Traditionally they have been given names beginning with J in memory of Charles I who, in his secret correspondence from the castle, referred to himself as 'J'. Formerly buried in the grounds of the castle, they are now retired to the Donkey Sanctuary at Sidmouth in Devon. Carisbrooke is probably the only well driven by donkey power in Europe.

When the Duke of York visited Carisbrooke, he was so impressed by the temperament of one donkey that he ordered he should have a penny loaf a day for life.

Specify, winner of the Grand National in 1971, was retired to Farringford House at Freshwater, then the property of his owner, Sir Fred Pontin. A plaque in the grounds records his life.

Jeddah, winner of the 1898 Derby, is commemorated in the hamlet of New Village at Freshwater. The house bearing his name was formerly the village forge.

A fourteenth-century assessment for providing horses for the war effort records that Godshill church were required to provide three, while and Brading and Newchurch, had to supply two each.

Perhaps it was appropriate that Mr Ernest Cottle should die from a heart attack while separating two fighting dogs. Ernest, a specialist in dermatology, moved to the Island in 1909 and took up residence in the family estate at Ningwood. He was honorary consultant physician at the Royal Isle of Wight Hospital at Ryde. In his spare time he devoted himself to raising Jersey cows and looking after the welfare of animals. When he died, he left land to be a Home of Rest for Horses. It continued until 1977, when the retired animals were moved to the mainland. To his wife he left the right to live at Ningwood until her death, £20 per annum – and a parrot.

There are more horses per acre on the Island than anywhere else in the United Kingdom (Newmarket excepted).

Wildlife
The zoo at Sandown occupies the site of old Granite Fort. In its early days the famous white tigers were a regular sight on the beach, going for a swim with their owner. Today, 'health and safety' would never allow it.

The Island is one of the few sanctuaries of the red squirrel. The arrival of their American cousins, the grey, has driven their smaller cousins out of much of Britain. The greys have been refused a passport to come to the Island and the natives are thriving.

The Island has its own unique butterfly, the Glanville Fritillary, named after a seventeenth-century entomologist, Lady Eleanor Glanville. Eleanor's life was less than happy. Twice married, her hobby was regarded as lunacy by her family and her son disputed her will.

There are seventeen species of bat in the United Kingdom, fourteen of which can be found on the Isle of Wight.

In *A View of the Isle of Wight in Four Letters to a Friend,* John Sturch in 1764 wrote how in the summer months an incredible number of exotic birds nested on the cliffs at Freshwater. He was greatly distressed by the local youths who were lowered down the cliffs with nooses [at great risk to themselves], to catch the birds, whilst others took to the water to shoot at them. In an open letter he wrote: 'Gentlemen, you should consider that what is sport to you, is death to us and our helpless orphans also.'

In praise of the nightingale, George Brannon, in his *Picture of the Isle of Wight*, wrote: 'to those visitors from the north, who perhaps never heard the unrivalled notes, the opportunity would prove not the least gratifying in a day's pleasure. On fine evenings in the months of May and June, the woods and groves in every direction resound with the delightful chorus of their inimitable songs.' Would that it was still so!

Henry Williamson, famous for his story *Tarka the Otter*, also wrote of a cormorant, a bird generally detested by fisherman. Because of its dark appearance it was known as an 'Isle of Wight Parson'.

At Sandown dancing bears provoked a flurry of high feeling; 'GHRD' wrote to the local paper in 1891 complaining of the danger of allowing bears to perform on the highway, causing horses to panic and risking accidents. Shortly afterwards, Maud Tomlinson related in her diary that a bear had killed his keeper and escaped into Sandown High Street – although whether she was confusing this with an incident in Devon is uncertain.

In 1905, the first ever kiang to reach Britain set hoof at Parkhurst Barracks. A kind of wild ass, it was captured in Tibet by the Mountain Artillery Battery Gunners and brought back to England. Its companion drowned en route. Later it was transferred to London Zoo. The only kiangs to be found in the British Isles today are at the Highland Wildlife Park in Scotland.

Before 1870, eagles were reported to be nesting at Culver and adding a Mediterranean touch, lizards are to be found among the rocky cliffs at la Falaise and the main car park in Ventnor.

Isle of Wight Bee Disease
In 1904 it was noticed that the bee population of the Island was suffering from some disorder. The bees exhibited distended abdomens and could only fly a few yards. Inside the hive those still alive clustered around the queen and she was the last to die. It was identified as being caused by a parasite. This same condition is today threatening the world population of bees.

Rescued at Sea
When the ship *Underley*, bound for Australia, hit rocks off Bonchurch and broke up, everyone on board escaped except for the Steward, who made a fatal attempt to rescue his canary.

The ship *Pomone*, serving in the Mediterranean, was nearly home when it grounded on Goose Rock in 1811 when taking a shortcut through the Needles. On board was Sir Harford Jones, carrying important papers relating to the war. On the way back they had stopped to collect the British Ambassador to Persia and he brought with him three stallions, a present from the Shah to King George III. Local vessels came to the rescue and the crew of 284 men were safely brought ashore. Then, at low tide, the horses were manhandled through the gun ports and managed to reach the beach but the loss of his ship was said to be more than the captain could bear.

The writer Henry Fielding was making what turned out to be his final journey to Portugal in 1754 in search of better health. Sheltering from a storm off Ryde, he was amazed when a flurry onboard ship revealed that one of four kittens retained to catch rodents had fallen into the water. Immediately the boatswain stripped off and dived into the turbulent sea. Fielding recorded that 'had the kitten had nine thousand instead of nine lives, I concluded that they had been all lost.' In this he was wrong and minutes later the boatswain emerged carrying the kitten in his mouth. The creature appeared to be dead and the captain, touched by the loss, declared that he would rather have lost a cask of brandy – a view not shared by the crew, who were superstitious about having cats on board. The story however had a happy ending, for after exposure in the sun the kitten made a complete recovery.

SOME GEOGRAPHY

COAST

The Island is definitely getting smaller. Land-slips, cliff falls and tidal erosion are all chipping away at the edges.

The original Needles rock was about 100ft tall. It fell during a storm in 1764, leaving behind something resembling a set of molars.

Observers braving the cold weather in February 1799 witnessed what appeared to be an optical illusion as Pitlands Farm, near to Blackgang, seemed to be moving. Within minutes there was a mighty roar as the farm and about 100 acres of land disappeared into a 40ft-deep chasm, killing two people. A farm cottage also disappeared into the abyss, only its chimney showing. It was believed to have landed still standing on its foundations.

One of the biggest falls was in 1928, when 100,000 tons of rock and debris tumbled towards the sea near Blackgang Chine, closing forever the historic coach road to Niton. It is still worth walking along what remains of the road, for the impact is awesome.

In 1935, 1,000 tons of rock also slid seawards in a landslide, while thousands more tons of rock fell 200ft onto the beach at Blackgang in 1978.

Residents of Freshwater Bay woke in up in 1968 to discover that during a cliff fall a chalk stack had broken away from the cliff and the Mermaid Rock was born. On 25 October 1992, however, the Arch Rock at Freshwater Bay suddenly collapsed, leaving a void.

The rock named the Stag got its name because a deer being hunted made a desperate leap onto the rock to escape the hounds. Is it too much to hope that they let it go?

A Tourist Tradition

There are twenty-one different coloured sands in the cliffs at Alum Bay – a world-beating range. The only colour that does not occur naturally is blue. Not noticing this, the Victorian writer George Eliot waxed lyrical about 'the rainbow of brightest maize, violent, pink, blue, red, brown and brilliant white, worn by the weather into a fantastic fretwork...it seems an enchanted place.'

In 1760, Josiah Wedgwood was experimenting with the use of Alum Bay sand for making pottery and by the 1780s Benjamin Sobell, 'table dresser' to King George III, had found a way of fixing the sands to surfaces thus starting a fashion for sand pictures. They sold outside Carisbrooke Castle for between 1/- and 2/6d (5p, 12½p). Filling pots with coloured sand continues today.

Between the chairlift and the Needles Rocks about a mile away, the cliffs date from 35 million to 65 million years BC.

LIGHTHOUSES, LEDGES AND LANDMARKS

Shine a Light!

It was James Walker, a Scottish engineer, who built the Island's two lighthouses at the Needles and St Catherine's point. Earlier lighthouses had failed, frequently obscured when they were most needed – by fog. Walker, who worked as a consultant to Trinity House, came up with two different designs.

His first attempt at St Catherine's in 1838 turned out to be too high, the light lost in the fog, so the tapering tower was lowered by 13m. Lit by oil lamps, there was a further problem of misting the glass.

It took Michael Faraday to develop a siphon chimney to draw off the oil residue. It went into operation in 1840 and the light, equivalent of 6 million candles, reaches for up to 30 nautical miles. In 1997 the lights were automated and the foghorn dispensed with. The next landfall after St Catherine's – would be in South America!

The Needles light was placed on the furthest of the chalk stacks in 1855, dug into the rock. The tower was built of granite. Five storeys high, it is nearly 73ft to the gallery, having a diameter of 21ft, and was manned by three men. It was a hazardous business getting out to the rock in rough weather. In 1994 the light was automated and lighthouse keepers became a thing of the past. A new system of fog signal was also introduced. The Needles light reaches up to 17 nautical miles and is the equivalent of 35,000 candlepower.

All the lighthouses around the British Isles are now operated from a central point in Harwich.

Round the Edges

The Isle of Wight coastline is approximately 60 miles. The sea around the coast is wild and unpredictable. Of the Solent, in Saxon times the Venerable Bede warned that: 'In this sea two ocean tides which break upon Britain from the boundless northern ocean meet daily in conflict beyond the mouth of the river Hamble which enters the same sea. When their conflict is over they flow back into the ocean whence they came.' Approaching the Island shores was always hazardous.

There are thirty named bays, in alphabetical order being: Alum Bay, Binnel, Brighstone, Brook, Chale, Colwell, Compton, Freshwater, Gurnard, Horseshoe, Luccombe, Monks, Mounts, Newtown, Orchard, Osborne, Priory, Reeth, Sandown, Scratchels, Seagrove, Steel, Thorness, Totland, Ventnor, Watcombe, Watershoot, Wheelers, Whitecliff and Woody.

There are also twenty separate chines (natural fissures in the cliffs) leading to the sea: Alum Bay, Barnes, Blackgang, Brambles, Brook, Chilton, Churchill, Compton, Cowleaze, Grange, Ladder, Linstone, Luccombe, New, Shanklin, Shepherd's, Shippards, Walpen, Whale and Widdick.

Numerous caves surround the Island's coast. At Bonchurch, Old Jack is said to have frequently held 500 tubs of smuggled brandy, while at Freshwater Cliffs, Frenchman's Hole got its name from the legend that a French fugitive hid there and died of starvation. Below Tennyson Down are Neptune's Caves at 200ft deep, Bat Cave 90ft in depth and Roe Hall, said to be 600ft high. Two other caves take their names from the Island's Governor, Sir Robert Holmes, being known as his Parlour, where he allegedly entertained guests, and the Cellar where he stored wine.

A cave at Watcombe Bay is listed 69th in the world's longest sea caves. Culver Cliff boasts the Nostrils and Hermit's Hole, while Brighstone has Dutchman's Hole and Luccombe boasts a cave that was regularly used by smugglers.

Yachting

The first recorded yacht race at Cowes was held on 10 August 1826, thought up by the Earl of Yarborough, a Lincolnshire man who had the good fortune to inherit Appuldurcombe House at Wroxall. It made a perfect base for his seafaring activities. The race was open to any gentleman who owned a yacht of at least 10 tons and was the beginning of an annual event, scheduled for the first week of August – to follow on from the social gatherings at Goodwood Races.

Only the aristocracy could take part, the epithet Royal being added when the Prince Regent took an interest. Thereafter, William IV, the Sailor King, named it the Royal Yacht Squadron. King Edward VII and George V were avid sailors, along with Edward's nephew Wilhelm, future Kaiser of Germany.

In 1857, an international trophy was put forward to be challenged for by any two yacht clubs. The prize, a jug in fine ornate silver, was originally called the Royal Solent Yacht Club trophy but the name was changed to the America's Cup, after the first winning yacht came from the New York Yacht Club. Thereafter, the two yacht clubs did battle for 125 years, the prize remaining relentlessly in American hands until 1983, when the Royal Perth Yacht Club threw down the challenge and wrested the Cup away from the Americans.

At the beginning of the twentieth century, Thomas Lipton, a self-made tea merchant and former cabin boy from Glasgow's Gorbals, regularly challenged for the America's Cup. In spite of his friendship with King Edward VII, being 'common', he was not invited to join the Royal Yacht Squadron until the end of his life – when he turned down the offer!

As more challenging races were thought up, the Fastnet Race became the most demanding – being a 608 miles dash from Cowes around the Fastnet Rock in the Irish Sea. The prize became known as the Admiral's Cup. Seven yachts took part in the first race in 1925 and, by 1978,

303 yachts lined up in stormy conditions. During that race seventeen people lost their lives, leading to a tightening up of entry qualifications.

Cowes Week attracts huge numbers every year, both 'yachties' and onlookers. Street entertainment, balls and fireworks turn it into a carnival.

In 1931, the Island Sailing Club set up a challenge for an international race around the Island. Taking place each June and covering 50 miles, competitors sail from Cowes to the Needles then back via St Catherine's Point. A spectacular sight, entries have now risen to over 1,800 yachts.

Sir Francis Chichester was the first and fastest man to circumnavigate the world in 1967, in his ship *Gypsy Moth IV*. Sir Francis expressed no sentiment about the ketch, saying that she was 'cantankerous and difficult,' and she was later laid up in dry dock and in increasing danger of deterioration. In 2002 she was bought by the UK Sailing Academy and brought to Cowes, where she was restored, becoming part of a maritime heritage exhibition.

Landmarks
Visiting about 1911, the poet Edward Thomas was all in favour of electing a local king who 'might turn his guns on the monuments of the Island,' viewing them as 'one form of tyranny.' In his view, they impeded the eye and detracted from the long procession of downs that are 'ancient Britain still.'

One offending item was the 341ft high Yarborough Monument, erected on Bembridge Down in 1849 and extolling the virtues of Charles Anderson Pelham, owner of Appuldurcombe House at Wroxall.

Another, the Alexandrian Pillar, is an impressive column topped by a globe, marking a visit by Tsar Alexander I of Russia to England in 1814. It is commonly known as the Hoy Monument, built on the orders of Michael Hoy, who grew rich from trading with Russia. Later, St Catherine's Down, on which the monument stands, was owned by William Henry Dawes, a soldier who fought against the

Russians at the time of the Crimean War and added his own memorial in praise of the Allies who died at Sebastopol.

The Ashey Sea Mark, erected on the high point of Ashey Down in 1735 by the navy, was a semaphore station used to relay messages from the Island to Portsmouth.

The Pepper Pot is all that remains of a thirteenth-century lighthouse and oratory built on St Catherine's Down as a penance by Walter de Goditon, who took cargo from a wrecked ship.

Sir Richard Worsley raised the Worsley Monument in 1747 in memory of his predecessor Sir Robert, who lived a 'long and exemplary life.' It stands on the highest point of the Worsley estate on Wroxall Down, now somewhat reduced, having been struck by lightning in 1831. Alas no more is Cook's Castle that once stood on the opposite side of the valley, a folly intended to enhance the view from Appuldurcombe House, the Worsley mansion at Wroxall. Cook's Castle may once have been occupied. It was a turreted mock castle, serving teas to walkers and charging 6*d* to climb the tower and enjoy the view.

Early Ships

Always a seafaring Island, many momentous voyages started from here. In 1663, two ships, the *Ark* and the *Dove*, set sail from Cowes furnished with a Charter from King Charles I to set up the state of Maryland. Aboard were 121 passengers. Women were very thin on the ground, numbering just three – Ann Cox, a gentlewoman and wife of Thomas Green Esq., Ann Smithson-Norman, travelling with her husband Robert, and Mary Jennings, who seems to have been alone. Three hundred years later a plaque was erected along Cowes Parade to record the event.

HMS *Sirius* set sail for Australia with the First Fleet on 13 May 1787. She reached Sidney 250 days later. The ship then set off on a second voyage to secure provisions for the fledgling colony, returning there on 19 June 1789. Her third sortie was to be her last for at Norfolk Island she ran aground and was wrecked on 26 January 1788. A plaque close to the Appley Tower at Ryde marks her departure point.

THE END OF THE PIER?

Piers were the darlings of the Victorians. Apart from a practical use as landing stages, the pleasure pier allowed tourists to take to the water without danger of seasickness. During both world wars, the piers were disabled to prevent enemy landing and their fortunes fluctuated. Only four remain on the Island.

Ryde

The first and most important was Ryde Pier. Opened in 1814, it allowed, for the first time, ship's passengers to avoid the indignity of being carried across the sands to the ship on a porter's back! A second pier opened alongside it in 1864 for a horse-drawn tram to carry pedestrians the length of the structure and in 1880, the railway line was extended to the pier head. Not wishing to be left behind as a leisure resort, a pavilion was erected in 1895.

Philip Norman's iconic novel *Babycham Nights* is set around the skating rink that once graced the structure. The pier is now a Grade II listed building.

Sandown

In the 1890s Sandown seafront was a hive of summer entertainment. Punch and Judy shows, a coconut stall, ice-cream barrows, Donald Marshall and his Royal Osborne Minstrels (complete with blackened faces), donkey rides and controversial dancing bears all vied for audiences. The original Sandown Pier opened for business in 1879 but at only 360ft long it was soon extended and enhanced with a pavilion.

Its history was rocky and interrupted by war. In 1934 Earl Jellicoe opened the newly furbished pavilion and in 1965, Lord Louis Mountbatten was installed as the Island's Governor, the ceremony taking place on the pier. The Queen and Prince Philip then departed from the landing stage. The pier's variety show included performances by Sir Harry Secombe, Gene Pitney, Pam Ayres, Bob Monkhouse, Frankie Howard and Lennie Henry, but, following a fire, the pavilion closed in 1999. The pier however still provides seaside entertainment.

Yarmouth Pier

At 809ft long, Yarmouth Pier is the longest wooden pier in the UK, built adjacent to Yarmouth Castle in 1876. Used as a promenade and popular with fishermen, it was refurbished in the 1990s and is still operational.

Totland

Totland Pier opened in 1879 in the expectation of regular visits by pleasure steamers. It was built at the same time as the Totland Bay Hotel, part of an ambitious plan to turn Totland into a genteel seaside resort. It was only partly successful. Coastal erosion and, later, vandalism, sees the pier continue to deteriorate. There is a café close to the shore but the pier is closed to pedestrians. Hopefully a miracle (or a billionaire) might take pity on it. The Totland Bay Hotel failed to meet health and safety regulations and was pulled down. Of his visit to the West Wight, John Betjeman declared: 'One feels that Western Wight is an earthquake poised in mid explosion.'

Gone but not Forgotten

Spare a thought for Shanklin Pier, 1,200ft long, with iron girders and wooden decking that opened in 1890. An elegant hydraulically-operated lift was also installed to carry visitors up the cliff to the town.

At its height, day trips were offered as far as Cherbourg. Before the First World War, a pavilion was installed and among the great performing there were prima ballerina Alicia Markova and American bass singer Paul Robeson. In 1918 the pavilion was burned down but, like a phoenix the pier kept rising from the ashes until, on the night of 15/16 October 1987, a hurricane swept it away.

A similar fate met Seaview Pier, one of only two suspension piers in the country. An elegant structure with four artistic towers, it was visited by the future King Edward VII and Queen Alexandra. The company having just bought its own steamer, the *Alleyn*, the First World War broke out, damaging its fortunes. Just when its artistic merit was recognised and it was granted protected status, on Boxing Day 1950 a hurricane of such force brewed that it blew the lovely structure away.

9

HEALTH AND CLIMATE

Health
The Island has a reputation for being a healthy place. Writing in 1860, the Revd Venables announced that: 'Invalids who resort to the Isle of Wight for warmth and shelter, naturally choose the winter months.'

Dr James Clark, physician to Queen Victoria, confirmed the therapeutic qualities, commenting on the 'several peculiarities of climate and position that render it a highly favourable residence for invalids throughout the year.'

Straight from the horse's mouth was a report from the Committee of the Royal Medical and Chirugical Society of England. In 1895 they declared that:

> Many classes of delicate persons are sent here with benefit: weakly scrofulous children, former residents of the tropics, adolescents with threatening or incipient tuberculosis of the lungs, old people and the large, heterogeneous group of individuals who, although structurally sound, cannot maintain their health excepting under specially favourable climatic conditions.

Still not feeling too well? Mr Alfred Greenham, wine merchant of Shanklin, can do you a nice line in Invalid Whiskey for 3/6d a bottle.

National Health Service?
A monk from St Mary's Priory was sent weekly to pray for the souls of the afflicted at Carisbrooke leper hospital. The exact site isn't certain but it was probably somewhere behind the cemetery at St Mary's, Carisbrooke, where there is a Priory Farm. Thankfully, by 1312 the inmates had dwindled to one. The Lady of the Wight, Isabella di Fortibus, gave one silver mark yearly towards its upkeep.

Around AD 1200, Willam de Vernon, Lord of the Island, for the good of his soul, donated land at Yarmouth to William Mackerel for making a hospital. In spite of French incursions, for some 500 years it survived, being known as The Refuge. Finally, in 1820, Daniel Alexander, architect of Dartmoor Prison, purchased the property and set about adding castellations and turrets, renaming it The Towers. The adjoining pathway is still called Refuge Lane. Daniel and his wife Anna Maria are buried in Yarmouth Church, where he donated 30ft of the tower to commemorate the death of his nineteen-year-old son Henry.

The Grim Reaper

In 1350 the Black Death threatened the Island. No one could leave without the king's permission. No grain could be exported and all shipping was controlled. This proved to be in vain, however, for much of the Island was decimated by the pestilence by 1352. Many villages were left deserted.

In 1583 the plague hit Newport, 200 persons dying from a population of 1,300. There being insufficient room to bury them at Carisbrooke, a new cemetery was opened at Church Litten.

In the nineteenth century, with the sudden influx of people who mattered, there was a rash of hospital building.

Ryde County Hospital opened its doors in 1849 with beds for twenty people. Children, the incurables and the insane were excluded. Patients were expected to wash their hands and faces every day. It provided free treatment for the needy plus paying beds. An outpatients' clinic opened then a laundry and, to celebrate Queen Victoria' Diamond Jubilee, a children's ward was added. Even with X-Rays, a nurses' home and a path lab, it was deemed unsuitable for modern treatment and closed in 1990.

The Royal National Hospital opened its doors along the Undercliff in 1869. The benign climate made Ventnor the ideal place for treating diseases of the chest. The building stretched for half a mile, consisting of about 100 individual, cell-like rooms. The hospital had its own market garden, farm and chapel. Treatment was mainly fresh air, rest and a good diet. In 1900 there were 148 patients but fifty years later there were 100 empty beds. The arrival of the NHS plus the discovery of drugs to treat TB made it redundant.

There were plans to turn it into a holiday camp but instead it was pulled down and Ventnor Botanical Gardens now occupies the site. The lovely stained-glass chapel windows by William Morris, Edward Burne Jones and Ford Maddox Brown were removed to St Lawrence Church.

Longford Hospital was the former retirement home of Joseph Rylands, wealthy industrialist and philanthropist at Havenstreet. When he left the Island, the house became an isolation hospital then a mental hospital. Today it is a Care Home, known as Northbrooke House.

Albany Barracks, at various times overflowing with the military, had its own hospital and three wells.

Lord Alverstone, a High Court Judge and MP for the Island, donated a hospital at Shanklin called Arthur Webster Hospital in memory of his twenty-eight-year-old son Arthur Webster, who died in 1902.

Scio Hospital was built at Shanklin, a gift from Mrs Julia Scaramanga-Ralli, the wealthy widow of Demetrius, a merchant, then living at Westhill House. It was erected in memory of her sons Peter and Eustatius. Intended as a surgical hospital for poor children it was called Scio, being the Italian name for the Greek Island of Chios. The Arthur Webster and Scio Hospital later amalgamated to form the Shanklin Cottage Hospital.

Whitecroft Hospital, the Island's 'County Lunatic Asylum', opened its doors in 1896 in the countryside, removed from centres of population. Prior to its opening, those with incurable psychiatric disorders were shipped to the mainland to a hospital at Knowle, in Hampshire. As part of the Care in the Community policy, the hospital closed in 1992. The beautiful Italianate bell tower has been listed by English Heritage.

In 1893 the Frank James' Memorial Seamen's Home opened, dedicated to their brother by John and William James. While exploring in West Africa, Frank wounded an African elephant that fought back and killed him. The ornate building in brick and terracotta was intended to house twelve single seamen but instead accommodated wounded soldiers returning from the Boer War. Later it became a cottage hospital and convalescent home. Shamefully, it has since been allowed to deteriorate – a piece of local history abandoned to its fate.

On visiting in 1869, J. Redding Ware reported that the Isle of Wight is the paradise of bees, flowers and invalids.

Cowes Doctor W. Hofmeister saved the life of a young lad, 'Harwood', after he fell from the quay at Cowes on 13 October 1870. It took two hours to revive him with the use of his galvanic battery.

During an outbreak of polio in 1950, swimming pools were closed and the opening of schools after the summer holidays delayed. In all, about 100 people were affected but only three died.

Water Water Everywhere?

When touring the Island in 1793, Henry Wyndham noted that:

> Such sometimes, though rarely, has been the scarcity of water in the neighbourhood of Cowes, that the poor part of the inhabitants has been known to arrest and empty the water-carts, on their passage to the town, in the same violent and outrageous manner, as if a famine should compel them to plunder either meat or bread, for the immediate satisfaction of their craving necessity.

On an altogether more sombre note, four workmen at Shanklin died, overcome by fumes as they laboured at the water works.

Carisbrooke Castle's well water was highly praised in 1802. To the palate it 'produces sensations of the most pleasing and agreeable nature. It has been taken to the West Indies, and on its return found perfectly good.'

The Shanklin Aerated Water Company came with the highest recommendation. Mr Otto Hehmer FIC, FCS, etc., analyst for the Isle of Wight County Council, speaking of the water supply, said 'a rapid and microscopical examination prove the entire absence of animal or vegetable life in any form. A purer and better supply could not be wished for.'

Spoilt for Choice
In 1833, Ryde offered a choice of Kemp's Hot or Cold Baths near to the pier or Rayner's Baths in Pier Street. Not excuse for being dirty.

Taking the Waters
It wasn't only Bath and Buxton that attracted visitors looking for relief from various ailments. The Island had its share of water-containing minerals that were supposedly good for the health.

The value of chalybeate springs was early recognised by Dr Fraser, physician to King Charles II – the water being rich in mineral salts of iron oxide.

In 1807, Dr Thomas Laurence Waterworth, a surgeon at Parkhurst Barracks, discovered a chalybeate spring near to Rock Cottage at Blackgang. Rich in iron he declared it to be beneficial for the treatment of dyspepsia, scrofulous diseases and 'passive haemorrhage of every kind.' He built a grotto offering the precious water for sale. Seeing its potential, Mr Cull of Newport promptly bought Rock Cottage and, by 1818, it had metamorphosed into the Sandrock Hotel. Among the visitors struggling to the remote spot was the future Queen Victoria and her mother, the Duchess of Kent, allowing the name Royal to be added. In 1815 the *Gentleman's Magazine* confirmed that the Island was a 'most desirable place for the resort of invalids.'

The innkeeper at the Sandrock declared that tea brewed from the water resembled ink and that it was good for boot blacking.

The fad for taking the waters did not last and a landslide destroyed the grotto at the Sandrock but the hotel struggled on until 1984, when a fire consumed it. Among its famous guests was Guiliemo Marconi, who carried out his transatlantic wireless tests at nearby Knowle Farm. The site of the Sandrock is now a housing estate. Dr Waterworth is buried in St Andrew's Church at Chale.

A similar spring was discovered at Shanklin, the water tinctured with alum. As a result, the Royal Spa Hotel was the first to be built along Shanklin Esplanade. *Shanklin Spa: A Guide to the Town*, published in 1903, extolled its 'Continental Winter Gardens and lounge, perfect cuisine' and assured that it was 'patronised by royalty of almost every European country. All the principal rooms faced the sea and it was lighted by electricity throughout. Apart from the dining, smoking and billiard rooms, there was a spacious livery that could supply coaches, while accommodation was afforded to motorists.

The adjoining baths opened in 1900 and had a complete system for all kinds of 'Hydropatical treatment.' It was not cheap. Double rooms were 4/- while a sitting room was a further 5/-. Breakfast cost 2/6, lunch 1/-, dinner 4/-, a fire in the room an extra 1/- and additional

wax candles 6*d*. Servants and children were accommodated at 6/- per day.

By 1900, when the water supply for Shanklin had become inadequate and 'a beautiful spring of water was purchased at Wroxall, brought into Shanklin, and runs by gravitation into the water mains of the town', it was confidently claimed that 'Shanklin water is purity itself'.

Man of All Work?

Advertisement from the 1860s: Gloucester House, High Street, Cowes. C M Kernot MD…Surgeon, Accoucheur, Cupper, Dentist &c. Medical Electricity and Galvanism performed. Chemical Preparations for Philosophical Amusements. Catalogue Gratis. [In a plain envelope?]

He also advertised 'A Fine collection of Human Anatomy on Sale.' Galvanism was a treatment to stimulate muscles through electric currents named for Luigi Galvani of Bologna (1737-1798), who discovered that the legs of dead frogs twitched when touched with a spark. He was dissecting the legs in the belief that that was where a frog's testicles were stored.

Mellowing with Old Age?

Queen Victoria was violently against smoking but when her granddaughter, Princess Victoria of Hesse, became a lifelong smoker, the Queen unbent sufficiently to give it a try.

And if all else Fails?

Island churchyards being nearly full, Ryde opened its first municipal cemetery in 1842 with 1 acre of land. The burial ground now covers 11 acres. Northwood cemetery had its first burials in 1856, while Shanklin and Ventnor provided new municipal cemeteries.

Springwood Woodland cemetery opened in 1995.

The Island's Crematorium opened in 1961 and the first year saw 308 cremations. Since then the figure has risen to about 1,400 per year. In case you wondered, you can't be cremated on Sunday, Christmas Day, Good Friday or a Bank Holiday – or preferably if you're still alive!

Keeping Fit with the Latest Fashion?

Dr Dabbs, amateur journalist, noted that, 'I saw a cyclist wearing the other day what he called a Ceylon flannel shirt. It seemed to me the very perfection of such a garment. I am told its price is about half a guinea.'

At the same time, Mr Redfern of Cowes did a nice line in tennis dresses in serge and wool.

10

MILITARY MATTERS

Today the Island is all peace and light but during its history it has been invaded, fought over, billeted and fortified.

Invasion!
Cerdic and his son Cynric arrived around AD 530, 'slaying many men' and leaving the Island to their nephews Stuf and Wihtgar, who were Jutes.

About AD 660, Wulfhere of Mercia 'ravaged the Isle of Wight', leaving Aethelwealh of the South Saxons in control.

In AD 686, Caedwalla, King of Wessex, set about exterminating the native population. The local king Aruald (think Steptoe) was slaughtered and his two brothers betrayed and killed, thus wiping out the Isle of Wight royal family. Aruald and his son are reputedly buried on Shalcombe Down.

The Danes came in AD 1001, laying waste to Newtown, then the biggest settlement. They camped at Werrar along the Medina, led by Swein, whose name survives at Swainston.

In 1066 the Normans set the pattern for centuries of squabbles. The French made repeated attacks along the coast, finally destroying Newport in 1377 after which 'no tenant was resident there for two years.'

Fighting Back
The Islanders didn't take it all lying down. A fleet went from Yarmouth in 1321 to Carlisle when the king was having a bust-up with Scotland. Three years later more ships set out from Yarmouth to transport troops to Aquitaine. Newport and St Helens were ordered to send fully equipped ships with men and arms to Portsmouth.

In 1335 the Island arrayed all able-bodied men, the best being sent to serve the king.

Paying for it All

Edward III set off in 1346 to invade Normandy with 1,000 ships and 4,500 bowmen. The Island contributed thirteen ships and 222 seamen from a population of about 4,500. All free men had to provide their own weapons while landowners were 'bound to defend the Castle of Carisbrooke' for forty days, at their own expense. All merchant shipping leaving Yarmouth was charged a levy of 6*d* in the £1 on merchandise, the money used to purchase warships. War doesn't come cheap!

Persistent Francais

The French landed about 1,000 men in 1403, capturing flocks and herds. A year later they returned and the Islanders offered a ransom as a delaying tactic in the hope of support from the mainland, but the French smelt 'un rat' and left again.

A Noble Effort?

Edward de Woodville, Captain of the Island, set off from St Helens in 1488 with forty gentlemen and 400 commoners. Their mission was to assist the Duke of Bretagne against the French King Charles VIII in a power struggle for Brittany. In the ensuing battle of St Aubin the Bretons were routed and only one Islander survived, a boy who returned to deliver the news.

Both Shanklin and Bonchurch claim the credit of killing Chevalier d'Eulx, commander of a French ship that made the mistake of landing on a deserted beach in 1545 in search of water. Taking time to look around, the interlopers were set upon by the militia.

Where did he come From?

To help the Island's war effort, a nun from Amesbury donated a knight. On the same day, the Island's own knights were arrayed, totalling twenty-nine.

Fifteen hundred Scottish soldiers were billeted on the Island in 1527 because there was no money to send them home. Discipline broke down completely and for a year they terrorised the natives, committing mayhem and murder. Sir John Oglander despaired because their officers had appalling table matters. They finally withdrew, leaving a trail of red-headed infants in their wake.

Time to get out the Spanish Dictionary?

It was all hands to the pumps in July 1588 as 2,000 troops and Islanders prepared to take on the Spanish Armada, but as they watched, the flotilla drifted on by.

By the Sword Divided

After some initial excitement, the Civil War largely passed the Island by. The five royalist-held castles quickly succumbed to the parliamentary forces. Islanders armed with sticks supported the Roundheads and captured Carisbrooke. After some bluster, Cowes and Yarmouth surrendered, while Captain Brutus Buck, in command of Sandham Castle, popped out for some fresh air and returned to find in his absence that his men had surrendered. The little fortification at Gurnard was a pushover. Thereafter, the main complaint from Islanders was that they were expected to cough up cash and goods for the mainland when there was precious little protection offered to them.

Things changed in 1648 when King Charles inconveniently found himself locked inside Carisbrooke Castle. Thereafter, government troops arrived in droves, expecting invasion from all quarters to steal away the renegade monarch. Impatient with the king's prevarication, a group of parliamentary soldiers finally marched him off to the mainland in November 1648. Within two months he was shorter by a head.

After the drama of the Civil War, Yarmouth Castle mouldered quietly away. Visiting in 1794, Henry Wyndham concluded that it is 'now a useless building but affords a comfortable sinecure to the person who may be fortunate enough to be appointed the Captain.'

Lock Up Your Daughters!

Albany Barracks opened its doors in 1798 as the aftermath of the French Revolution threatened Britain. The site covered 20 acres and housed 2,040 men. A word of warning was issued: 'much as their military uniforms tend to enliven the dullness of a country town, the moral effects of such a congregation of the young and thoughtless, on the people of Newport, are very undesirable.'

Who Needs Enemies?

In 1793, the Grand Old Duke of York commandeered a contingent of troops from Hess to join the fight against the revolutionary French. The shame of it was that although they were British Allies, being labelled aliens they were not permitted to land. They arrived at Spithead in January 1794 and within two weeks, eighty-three horses trapped on board the ship died. Within a month, 641 men fell sick and between March and April, eighty-two men and two women died. When it was too late, they were grudgingly allowed ashore for short periods, the sick housed in draughty, unheated buildings. The victims were buried in Whippingham churchyard.

Bringing Out the Big Guns!

Brading acquired a town gun in 1549, a brass weapon created by 'brethren' John and Robert Owine. Installed in a special house in the grounds of the St Mary's Church, in 1588 it was hauled onto Culver Down, ready to repel the Spanish. In the event it was not fired. It remained in a virginal state for 300 years until it was decided to mark the passing of the Reform Bill in 1832 with a glorious celebration. The shock was too much for the old gun and it blew up.

Stolen in 1950 it was auctioned and returned to Nunwell House, where it remains despite requests for its return to its original place. Brighstone's Parish Gun took on an altogether more peaceful incarnation in 1740, being re-cast into a church bell.

Suicide Bomber?

On the day that King Charles declared war on his subjects at Nottingham, a Captain Wheeler was despatched to Yarmouth Castle to demand its surrender. The castle's commander, John Burley, had already refused to hand it over without written permission from the king. When Wheeler returned he found that Burley had placed barrels of gunpowder at each corner and had worked himself into a lather, announcing that he would rather die a thousand deaths than surrender. Having been given time to calm down – he surrendered.

Fear God and Honour the King!

When the same Captain Burley learned that King Charles had been locked inside Carisbrooke Castle he marched into Newport, purloined the town's drum – the property of the mayor – and called on the people to rescue their monarch. The Mayor, a staunch Parliamentarian named Moses Read, came to demand his drum back and when Burley refused, he was arrested and sent to trial at Winchester, where he was found guilty of treason. Technically this was impossible as he was campaigning for and not against the king but on 3 February 1648 he was hanged, drawn and quartered.

Conduct Unbecoming

During the seventeenth-century second Dutch War, Matthew Phripp, stationed with local forces on the Island, was accused of abusing his position and stealing prize goods.

Big Bertha

At Calbourne Mill, a mammoth 19ft 2in gun weighing 38 tons fronts the roadway. Installed at Cliff End Fort (also known as Fort Albert), its purpose was to guard the narrow opening between the Island and the Needles Channel. When it was tested in 1878, the resulting explosion caused so much damage to the fort that part of it had to be rebuilt. It was never actually used.

At the outbreak of the First World War, Kaiser Wilhelm's brother, Prince Heinrich of Prussia, was taking the waters at the Spa Hotel at Shanklin. He quickly left in a taxi driven by Mr Sid Hackett.

Victoria Cross Winners

The medal 'for valour' was introduced in 1856 but backdated to include acts of heroism during the Crimean War. Hancock the Jewellers in Burlington Arcade, London, make them from a cannon captured from the Russians at the siege of Sebastopol.

Island winners include:

William Thomas Rickard – a Ryde man who, in 1855, destroyed a Russian forage store, rescuing a fellow seaman from the mud. He served in the Island's coastguard service and is buried at St James's Church, Ryde.

Major Henry Tombs of the Bengal Horse Artillery, who twice rescued a fellow officer during the Delhi Siege. He later became a Major General and is buried at Mountjoy cemetery in Newport.

Colonel Henry George Gore Brown spiked the guns threatening the British residency at Lucknow. He is buried at St Mary's Church, Brook.

Sir Samuel James Browne 'Sam Browne' – after whom a belt was named following the loss of his left arm in battle. Serving with the Lucknow Cavalry, he later became a General, settling at Ryde, where his cremated ashes are buried.

Reginald William Sartorius – born in Portugal, died in Cowes in 1907 having won the VC for rescuing a mortally wounded sergeant during the Ashanti Wars. He is buried in Hampshire.

Francis David Millett Brown, saved a wounded soldier at Narnoul, India in 1857. His army service ended when he was 'superfluous to requirements' in 1894 and he retired to the Island, where he died a year later.

Two gentlemen held at His Majesty's Pleasure at Parkhurst won the VC. Thomas Flynn is reputed to be the youngest recipient, being only fifteen-years-old at the time. He won the medal in 1857 for acts of bravery while serving in India. A year later he spent thirty-one days at Parkhurst.

William Mariner left the prison to join the army during the First World War, serving in France where he single handedly went into enemy territory to spike a German gun. He died a year later in France. He served his sentence under his original name, changing it on leaving prison.

Royal Regrets

Between 1886 and his death in 1895, Prince Henry, husband of Queen Victoria's youngest daughter, Beatrice, commanded the Isle of Wight Rifles. Stifled by his mother-in-law's demands, he escaped to Africa to take part in the Ashanti War, where he caught a fever and died. His body was shipped home to be buried at St Mildred's Church, Whippingham. His wife remained a widow for even longer than her mother.

After the First World War, Princess Beatrice, Governor of the Isle of Wight, had the duty of unveiling the war memorial at St Mildred's Church at Whippingham. The first name on the monument was that of her youngest son, Prince Maurice.

Prisoners of War

In 1947, while 700 German POWs were awaiting repatriation, 550 were treated to a concert party in the Medina cinema.

The Germans have Landed?

Contrary to claims that no German military set foot in Britain during the Second World War, a secret raid was allegedly carried out at St Lawrence in 1942. The target was the radar installation and in a lightning attack German soldiers scaled the cliffs then departed again for the Channel Islands. What they achieved is uncertain but to avoid panic the incident was hushed up. It may never have come to light had not at least one British soldier vanished. Officially he was thought to have fallen from the cliff and drowned, his body washed away. Imagine the joy when his family apparently received a postcard from a POW camp announcing that he was alive. Others are researching this interesting event so perhaps the truth will out?

HONOUR AMONG GENTLEMEN?

Whose Sword is it Anyway?

In 1741, two men, William Roach and Richard Newman, fell out over ownership of a sword. In the ensuing duel, they both died.

Pistols at Dawn

A duel was fought at Carisbrooke Castle in 1813. Two lieutenants based at Parkhurst Barracks had fallen out. Some weeks earlier John Blundell had married, asking his friend Edward McGuire to give the bride away, which he did. A little later, Blundell told several people that he had had to lend McGuire clothes to wear at the ceremony and McGuire was offended. The men were camped at Niton and their squabble at the White Lion pub turned nasty. Egged on by their companions, neither man could see a way out without losing face so on Friday 9 July, they, with their seconds, went to Carisbrooke and duly fired two shots at each other. McGuire's second shot fatally wounded Blundell, who died three days later. McGuire and the seconds were tried for murder, found guilty and sentenced to death. Happily, at the behest of the Prince of Wales, they were pardoned.

A Second Fatal Duel

In December of 1813 a fatal duel took place in Northwood Park. The deceased was Thomas Sutton, who planned to leave the following day on the vessel *Grace*, bound for South America. Also on board were Major Lockyer, Thomas Redesdale and a Mr Hand. The *Grace* was then seized by the Customs at Cowes for various discrepancies and because of the delay, the passengers retired to the Dolphin Inn.

At some point Sutton made a remark upsetting Lockyer, who immediately challenged him to a duel. Along with Redesdale and Hand they met the following morning at Northwood Park. Lockyer fired a single shot, hitting Sutton in the heart. He died immediately. The three remaining men promptly vanished. Tried in their absence, they were found guilty of murder. Mr Hand was later arrested in Newport but whether the others were ever caught is not known.

Famous Last Nights

General Wolfe spent his last night in England at St Cross in Newport, at the home of Joseph Fitzpatrick. Wolfe died on 13 September 1760 in the battle to claim Canada from the French, famously scaling the challenging Heights of Abraham to take the French unawares.

Sir John Moore spent his last night at Hazards House in Newport before sailing for Spain, where he died at Corruna in the Penninsular Wars against Napoleon. Hazards House, a seventeenth-century dwelling, was knocked down to make way for an extension to the County Hall.

Sad

During a muster on St George's Down on 3 July 1632, an unfortunate militiaman, Sampson Saphior, was accidentally shot. Having examined him, Sir John Oglander, as coroner, pronounced that: 'no skin was broken but certainly all the nerves and sinews in the poll of his head were either broken off or, with the fire, shrunk up and his brain turned in his head.'

Remembering the Dead

The Isle of Wight war memorial in St Nicholas Chapel at Carisbrooke Castle contains plaques recording all the military dead from both world wars, numbering 1,624. This includes the names of 526 men of the Isle of Wight Rifles, who died in the First World War.

The following towns and villages have war memorials: Arreton, Ashey, Bembridge, Binstead, Bonchurch, Brading, Brighstone, Calbourne, Carisbrooke, Chale, Cowes, East Cowes, Freshwater, Lake, Newchurch, Newport, Porchfield, Niton, Ryde, Sandown, Shanklin, St Lawrence, Thorley, Totland, Ventnor, Whippingham, Whitwell, Wootton, Wroxall and Yarmouth.

Godshill has a memorial garden while other parishes, villages and hamlets commemorate their dead via plaques, rolls of honour and memorial windows. Following extensive bombing at Cowes and East Cowes, both towns have civilian memorials. In total 214 non-combatants were killed. Other groups commemorated include firemen (thirteen died at Shanklin), lighthouse men (three killed at Niton) and officers and prisoners commemorated at Parkhurst – the latter are not recorded by name. A lychgate, an organ, central heating, houses and schools were all purchased to honour the dead.

The Blue School in Newport was opened in 1761 for the education of poor girls. After the Second World War it was renovated and became a war memorial.

Doing One's Bit for the War Effort
To help with food shortages in the Second World War, Freshwater Library sacrificed their lawns to grow cabbages. All was well until an invasion of great white butterflies left behind an army of greedy green caterpillars. Having consumed the cabbage banquet they then went in search of literary fulfilment, and unsuspecting customers found unwelcome, squashed bookmarks inside their chosen volumes.

In 1917, a Seed-Potatoes sub-committee was set up at Shalfleet Parish to distribute 25cwt of King Edwards and Arran Chiefs. Mr Rolfe, the Ningwood stationmaster, was in charge of weighing the potatoes.

The following year, 3 tons of spuds were supplied. By 1928 the enthusiasm for allotments had waned to the point where the scheme was abandoned.

Making the Ultimate Sacrifice?
In 1919, Dr Cottle of Shalfleet left much of his estate to the RSPCA to open a home for horses. With the outbreak of the Second World

War, the animals were destroyed so that their grazing could be used to grow food.

Island Ships in Active Service

In 1940, six ships from Newport Harbour set out for the dramatic rescue at Dunkirk.

The Island Ferries that did their bit during the First World War were:

Stirling Castle, built 1899, went into service with the Isle of Wight and South of England Steam Packet Company (Red Funnel) in 1907. She was employed as a minesweeper and in 1918 was lost at sea off the coast of Malta.

Princess Mary went into service in 1911 with Red Funnel ferries. She was damaged when she hit the wreck of HMS *Majestic* in the Mediterranean and sunk off the Dardanelles.

In 1917 the paddle steamer *Her Majesty*, along with the *Beatrice*, both served as minesweepers in the English Channel and the Irish Sea. On her return to service, *Her Majesty* was converted to a car ferry, carrying eighteen cars.

During the Second World War the Island ferries that did their bit were:

The PS *Portsdown* belonged to Southern Railways. Her task was to carry mail to the Island. In September 1941 she hit a mine and sank off Southsea. A year earlier she had evacuated hundreds of men from Dunkirk.

The PS *Whippingham* also picked up men from Dunkirk. Built to hold 1,000 men, she took on board 2,700, being so low in the water that she was barely afloat. She remained in service until 1962, when she was broken up.

PS *Ryde* and PS *Sandown* were both requisitioned as minesweepers saw service around Dover. *Ryde* also served as an anti-aircraft ship and was at the Normandy landings, but made it home and both vessels went back into service.

Ryde was finally withdrawn in 1968 and escaped breaking up, becoming instead a nightclub along the river Medina. Sadly, she has since been abandoned and is almost beyond rescue.

The Red Funnel ferries *Princess Helena* and *Solent Queen* both set out for Dunkirk but returned without picking up troops.

Southsea was sent to the north-east coast as a minesweeper but was herself mined and sunk on active service in the Tyne estuary in 1942.

The *Lorna Doone* saw active service in both world wars but when she was finally returned to Red Funnel, she was in such poor condition that the decision was taken to scrap her.

They also served those who stayed at home. Paddle steamer *Shanklin* did her bit for the war effort by remaining in passenger service from Ryde to Portsmouth. She was withdrawn from service in 1965.

In 1936, Red Funnel launched the paddle steamer *Gracie Fields*, the naming ceremony carried out by her namesake. The boat operated between Cowes and Southampton. In 1939 she was requisitioned for military service and sank during the Dunkirk rescue mission.

P.L.U.T.O.
Not Disney's delightful dog but an ambitious scheme to help the war effort by pumping oil from Shanklin to Cherbourg. The oil travelled from the mainland to Gurnard and then underground to Shanklin, where a huge reservoir, holding 620,000 gallons, pumped the precious supplies to the allies. The departure point was near Shanklin's now-vanished pier.

Coastal Forts
In the nineteenth century, in response to a perceived threat of French invasion, a series of coastal forts were commissioned. By the time they were completed the threat had abated. They were then dubbed Palmerston's follies after the Prime Minister.

On the Island the following forts were built between 1852 and 1937. Starting with the East Coast were batteries at Sandown Barracks,

Yaverland, Redcliff, Culver, Steynewood and Puckpool. There were also installations at Sandham Fort, Bembridge Fort and Nodes Point. On the West Coast were Fort Victoria, Fort Albert (also known as Cliff End), Fort Redoubt, Warden Point and Golden Hill, plus batteries at the Needles, Hatherwood and Bouldner.

In addition there are four circular forts built in the Solent, intended to guard the shipping lanes leading to the dockyard at Portsmouth. No longer necessary, they were offered for sale in the 1960s and three are in private ownership. The MOD retained control of Horse Sand Fort.

Spitbank Fort, completed in 1878, was in service until after the First World War. Among its various civilian roles were suggestions that it would be converted into a brewery. The original well was drilled 400ft into the seabed, providing pure water from the chalk, ideal for making beer. It featured in the television programme *Most Haunted* and the late television presenter Jeremy Beadle underwent imprisonment in the dungeons to see how he would cope.

St Helen's Fort was completed in 1880 and occasionally, at low tide, the original causeway is sufficiently exposed to enable group walks from St Helen's Church to the fortification.

In 1972, No Man's Land Fort was used in a *Dr Who* series called 'The Sea Devils'.

Brighstone Holiday Camp – the first to be built on the Island (1929-31) – was handed over to the military in 1939 and occupied by 1,000 soldiers.

East Cowes Castle, Totland Bay Hotel and Steephill Castle were among buildings commandeered to be used as military barracks or hospitals.

Air Crashes during the Second World War
The Island had the misfortune to be under the flight path of aircraft flying to and from France. It was also alarmingly close to two military targets at Portsmouth and Southampton.

In the course of the war sixty-five aircraft crash-landed on the Island, while others went down in the sea around the coast. Two thirds of those crashing were British and as a result of the accidents twenty-three men died, ten were injured and twenty escaped unscathed. Following German crashes, twenty-seven men died and twenty-one men were taken prisoner. Casualties were treated at Ventnor National Hospital.

While the main targets were on the mainland, enemy planes were not averse to dropping their bombs as they flew overhead. In total over 200 Island civilians died and nearly 600 were injured.

The worst sustained raid was on Cowes on the evening of 4/5 May 1942, when 160 German planes mounted an attack leaving at least seventy people dead. The youngest to die was five-week-old Peter Vivian Coster and the oldest, eighty-two-year-old Ellen Varney. William and Naomi Broadwater, who both perished, had been married for forty-two years and had a combined age of 155 years.

The casualties might have been worse had it not been for the presence of the Polish ship *Blyskawica* (Lightning) that was being refitted at J. Samuel White's shipyard and put up a counter-attack. A memorial to the ship stands in a shelter along the Parade at Cowes.

11

PLANES, BOATS, CARS AND TRAINS

ROADS

It may come as a surprise to Islanders, but according to the Revd Venables, writing in 1860, 'the Isle of Wight has been famed for the excellence of its roads.'

The Agricultural Survey of Hampshire confirmed that for 'the convenience of travellers ... this highly favoured spot is not to be surpassed by any part of Britain.'

The Island has 480 miles of roads and 515.8 miles of footpaths and bridleways.

In the nineteenth century there were fifty-two gates across the road between Newport and Yarmouth, requiring travellers to employ a boy to open and close them.

Not all was perfect however. In 1794, Henry Penruddock Wyndham warned of the perils of crossing Wootton Bridge: 'a narrow causeway, more than three hundred yards in length over which the high road passes from Newport to Ryde, and which, till lately, when there was no railing to it, was very terrific to the travelling passenger.' [It is interesting to see the word 'terrific' used in its original sense, as instilling terror.]

When travelling from Cowes to Yarmouth, Wyndham issued a word of warning: 'that the whole of this road is not suitable even for two wheel chaises'. And of routes in general: 'the roads are not to be undertaken in any sort of carriage except in the driest season'. Clearly it was wiser to ride or walk.

The 1813 Highways Act permitted the taking of a toll and fifty tollgates promptly sprang up to the chagrin of travellers, being finally removed by 1889.

In the nineteenth century, the journey from London to Portsmouth required seven changes of horses and took about twelve hours.

The traveller would have been encouraged by milestones, thoughtfully spelling out the distance still to cover. Of the hundreds that may once have been scattered around the Island, only a few remain. You will find some in the following places:

Chale has four, one on the corner by the church wall, one opposite Chale House, a third along Chale Street by the bridge, and a fourth in Town Lane.

At Limerstone marking 6 miles from Newport.

At Brighstone (in the wall of the tea gardens) announcing 7 miles to Newport.

In Newchurch outside Wisteria Cottage, recording 91 miles to London.

At Brading in the pavement opposite the turn to Morton Manor.

In Mersley Lane, Knighton, embedded in the farmhouse at the Garlic Farm.

On Forest Road, a borough marker along the bend of the road, on the left side heading for Newport.

The fastest journey to the Island was by mail coach, but it took only three passengers and travelled by night. The stagecoach was the equivalent of the bus service but wealthy people were wary of risking their valuables to highwaymen.

The roads were generally rough, potholed and, in winter, often a quagmire. The able bodied from the House of Industry were employed to fill in the holes.

By 1904 the Island boasted a motorised bus service – but the roads were so bad that it had to be abandoned, re-emerging after the First World War. The first physician from Ryde hospital to live outside the town was Dr S.V.H. Underhill. He was able to do so because, in 1908, he had a motor car.

Breaking the Speed Limit?

Noah Cooley was found guilty of driving a horse and carriage in a furious manner in Ventnor. He claimed that he was hurrying to overtake a coach as his passengers had missed it. A witness stated that he was not travelling above 9 miles per hour but he was fined one shilling with twelve shillings costs.

Bad Luck

The only Island man to die on the *Titanic* was Alfred Ernest Nicholson of Shanklin, who ran a tea business in New York. Leaving Mrs Nicholson behind, he planned to visit his sister, Mrs Ripley in New York; and so bought himself a first class ticket that cost him £26.

After the disaster, his body was picked up by the steamer *Mackay Bennet*. Some idea of his success can be seen by his possessions, which helped to identify him – a pearl scarf pin bearing the letter N, a gold watch and chain, a gold pencil, a diamond horseshoe-shaped pin, gold cufflinks, three gold studs and £9 in gold in his pocket book; clearly a man who liked 'bling'. Whether his wife wanted him back is a moot point because his sister had him delivered to her and he was buried in New York.

WATER

Rivers

Officially the Island has three rivers, the Medina (10½ miles), the Eastern Yar (17 miles) and the Western Yar (about 4 miles) although there are numerous other streams and tributaries. The creeks at Newtown and Yarmouth are tidal. The Medina is partly tidal and navigable only north from Newport.

Unusually, the Island rivers run from south to north. The Western Yar once flowed into the sea at Bembridge but the land around Brading has been largely reclaimed.

Ladies First

Ships are usually referred to as 'she' and have right of way over motor transport. The Yar Bridge Act confirmed this right in 1858. To avoid congestion in the summer, the Yarmouth Bridge (Western Yar) is opened for ten minutes every hour. In winter the Harbour Office requires half an hour's notice. The bridge operates marine signals: Red = Stop, Red and Green = Stand By and Green = Go. Hand signals from boats are not permitted!

In 1860 the first bridge was built over the Western Yar, connecting Freshwater to the rest of the Island. Before that, travellers had depended upon a ferry, started in 1706. The old wooden bridge had a single lane and operated a toll. In 1934 it was taken over by the Isle of Wight Council and the toll was abolished.

The Island is partially bisected by the River Medina and anyone wishing to cross from East to West Cowes once faced a 7½-mile journey around Newport. In 1859, a chain ferry crossing the Medina at Cowes started transporting both vehicles and pedestrians. Originally anyone wishing to make the crossing had to rely on a horse-drawn pontoon that was designed to transport both carriages and livestock. The present chain ferry can carry up to twenty cars and pedestrians and cyclists traditionally go free. It bears the uninspiring name *Five,* being the fifth to be operated by the local authority.

Getting off the Island

Until regular passenger companies were set up (around 1817), boats had to be summoned when needed. In 1802, a commentator assured visitors that at Ryde 'a vessel can be commanded to go off from Lower Ryde at any weather, or at any time of the tide, for which they can only demand 5/- , and boatmen are liable to a heavy fine for demanding more. The fare to Yarmouth is 6*d* although visitors are usually charged 1/-.'

CARS

In 1893, American inventor Henry House, who set up a factory at East Cowes to experiment with liquid gas as a fuel, was prosecuted for driving a horse-less carriage past Osborne House at 26 knots! He was fined £3 with 11/- costs. House, who had as early as 1866 invented a horse-less carriage carrying up to seven people and capable of speeds of 30mph, promptly closed his factory, making 200 local people redundant. Among his many innovations were paper plates and shredded wheat.

In 1900 there were twenty cars on the Island. An Act of Parliament for 1904 made the registration and displaying of number plates on cars obligatory. A year later, Mr Charles Edgar of Preston Place, Ryde, had the doubtful honour of being the first Island man to be convicted of drunk driving. He was accused of travelling down Ryde High Street in a 'reckless and furious manner,' and was fined £1 and had his licence suspended for three months.

The first Island car number plate was DL1. DL remained the Isle of Wight registration until 2001, to be replaced by HW that unites both the Isle of Wight and Hampshire.

The only traffic lights operating on the Island with two lights rather than three are at Carisbrooke Castle.

A van belonging to the Royal Blue Automobile Services knocked over a large tin of white paint at Shorwell on 11 September 1934. 'The driver accepted liability.' This momentous event was recorded in the Highway minutes.

RAILWAYS

On 3 September 1887, Joshua King of West Cowes, aged 3 years and 9 months, achieved an unhappy first when he died from injuries received by being knocked down by a railway engine.

Until 1845 local landowners blocked attempts to introduce the railway but 1862 saw the first line open from Cowes to Newport. The service was expanded in 1864, when the first line opened from St John's Ryde to Shanklin. In 1880 it was extended to Ryde Pier Head. Lines to Ventnor, Freshwater and stations in between followed.

The refusal of the Earl of Yarborough to allow the railway across his land meant that Ventnor Tunnel had to be excavated, taking two years to complete.

In its heyday, five companies served the Island, providing ferry links at Ryde, Southampton and Yarmouth. Southern Railway took over the rail network in 1923.

The Beeching Act fell on nearly all Island lines, leaving only Ryde Pier Head to Shanklin intact.

Enthusiasts rescued the route from Smallbrook Junction to Wootton in the 1960s, creating the Havenstreet Steam Railway.

The Islanders should have heeded the poet John Betjeman, who in 1952, broadcast a series of programmes on travel for the BBC. After a visit to the Island he wrote: 'Far too few people on the Isle of Wight have the sense to go by the railways. The fairest line goes from Cowes to Ventnor West. It was by this line that I, almost the only passenger, came to Ventnor.' If only we had the choice now.

AIRWAYS

An air show was held in 1929 at the aerodrome at Somerton, on the outskirts of Cowes. Somerton became an airbase during the Second World War. In the same year an aerodrome at Apse Heath, near Lake, opened, providing flights to the mainland.

The Island's favourite aircraft, the *Islander*, made its first flight in 1965. Designed by John Britten and Desmond Norman, it was a highly successful commercial plane based at Bembridge Airport. It was followed by a big brother, the *Trilander,* then the *Defender,* which had a military application.

Speed

Richard Noble OBE, a pilot, was involved in the development of the ARV Super 2 light two-seater aircraft at Sandown airport. The company went into administration and Noble pursued his dream of creating a 1,000mph car. The result was *Thrust 1* and *2*. With *Thrust 2*, a jet-propelled car, he held the world land speed record and was officially the first person to break the sound barrier. The record was then taken by *Thrust SSC*, reaching a speed of 763mph in 1997 in Nevada. Noble continues to work on *Bloodhound SSC* in pursuit of reaching the magic 1,000 miles per hour. The Island's airport at Sandown is still in operation.

The Island had a first with the 1965 launch of a Hovercraft passenger service from Ryde Esplanade to Southsea (crossing time 7 minutes). The prototype was built at Saunders Roe base at Cowes, where the Flying Boats had been developed. The hovercraft's designer was Sir Christopher Cockerell. The original 20ft vehicle, the first amphibious people carrier in the world, was dubbed *The Flying Saucer*. Early approaches to the airforce and navy came to nothing as the navy viewed it as a plane, and the airforce as a boat. Sir Christopher died in 1999.

When it became obsolete, the seaplane hangar based at Bembridge Harbour and used by both Royal and the US Navies was moved to Shanklin in 1923, to be used as an amusement arcade on the Esplanade.

12

ON THIS DAY ON THE ISLE OF WIGHT

1 January 1909
The first old age pensions were introduced. Thirteen hundred Islanders qualified.

2 January1945
The Greek ship *Varvasi* ran aground off the Needles. The ship's crew and cat, named Buddy, were all rescued.

22 January 1901
Queen Victoria died at Osborne House. Two artists, Emil Fuchs and Hubert Herkommer, rushed to Osborne to paint the Queen's corpse. Herkommer's portrait of the Queen surrounded by flowers and resembling Ophelia hangs outside her bedroom at Osborne.

23 January 1825
Albert Midlane, prolific hymn writer, was born at Newport. His most famous composition was 'There's a Friend of Little Children'. Midlane ran a hardware store in Newport and is buried at Mountjoy cemetery.

30 January 1649
King Charles was executed in London. Each year, on the anniversary, a service is held in the chapel of St Nicholas in the grounds of Carisbrooke Castle.

2 February 1843
Daniel Alexander, engineer, who designed London Docks and Dartmoor Prison, died and was buried in the family vault at Yarmouth.

5 February 1799
A hundred acres of land collapsed in a landslide at Pitlands Farm, burying buildings and killing two people.

6 February 1885
Edward Edwards, founder of the public library service, died at Niton
and was buried in the parish churchyard.

11 February 1908
Sir Vivian Fuchs, Antarctic explorer and scientist, was born in
Freshwater.

2 March 1907
The submarine *B2* ran aground in Sandown Bay while on exercises.
She was propped up with scaffolding poles until the next high tide,
when she was re-floated.

8 March 1996
Winifred Hastings, a Totland pensioner, announced her intention
to take 100 people on a flight on Concorde. Having no relatives
Winifred declared, 'I don't give a tinker's cuss who they are as long as
the government don't get their hands on my money.'

9 March 1907
About 200 poor and needy pensioners enjoyed a free meat tea at
Newport Drill Hall.

21 March 1931
A bramble fire spread to Ashey racecourse damaging the stands,
weighing-in rooms and jockey's dressing room.

26 March 1932
The UK's oldest steam locomotive, W 18 Ryde, built for the Isle of
Wight Railway, was put up for sale after travelling an estimated 1.5
million miles.

30 March 1912
The first twenty prisoners arrived at Camp Hill prison from Dartmoor.

30 March 1957
Following the introduction of petrol rationing, road accidents fell by
twenty per cent.

1 April 2009
The three Island prisons were amalgamated, to hold 1,700 prisoners.

2 April 1862
The ship *Cedrene,* bringing convicts back from the West Indies, foundered and the rescued men were taken to Brighstone. Here they drank the pub dry, got into a fight and troops from Parkhurst Barracks had to be summoned to quell the riot.

3 April 1876
Giuseppe Garibaldi arrived on the Island, staying at Brooke House with his friend Charles Seely.

9 April 2000
Charlie Kray, elder brother of the notorious twins, died in St Mary's Hospital. He was serving a twelve-year sentence at Parkhurst for smuggling cocaine worth £39 million.

15 April 1809
The poet Algernon Swinburne was buried at Bonchurch. His request that no religious ceremony should be held was largely ignored.

16 April 1817
John Keats arrived for the first of two visits to the Island, staying at Carisbrooke.

25 April 1586
Two Catholic priests, Roberton Anderton and William Marsden, were arrested when their ship ran aground. They were found guilty of landing illegally in England and were hanged, drawn and quartered after refusing to take an oath declaring that Queen Elizabeth was the head of the Church. In June 1933, bones discovered at Arreton Down were believed to be theirs.

28 April 1556
An Island gentleman, Captain Waddall, was taken to Tyburn, where he was hanged, drawn and quartered for his part in the Dudley Conspiracy, to de-throne Queen Mary. His head was displayed on Tower Bridge.

2 May 1660

Grace Hooke, niece of the scientist Robert Hooke, was born at Newport. She may have been the mother of Mary Holmes, the only acknowledged child of Sir Robert Holmes, the Island's governor. Mary married her first cousin Henry, when her father offered him his vast Island estates on condition that he did so. They produced sixteen children, most of whom died in infancy.

4/5 May 1942

Air raids over Cowes killed seventy people.

13 May 1835

John Nash, architect, died at East Cowes Castle and was buried in St James's Church.

29 May 1666

Sir Faithful Fortescue, Royalist, was buried at St Mary's, Carisbrooke.

6 June 1908

William Blake, owner of the Terminus pub in Ventnor, was fined £1 for having an automatic gaming machine.

16 June 1862

The first locomotive chugged its way along the new Cowes to Newport railway.

19 June 1920

Lord Gort, owner of East Cowes Castle, unveiled the East Cowes War Memorial. Gort led the British Expeditionary Force in the Second World War and won the Victoria Cross, dying in 1946.

28 June 1933

Prime Minister Ramsey McDonald was too busy to open 'Nansen Hill' on Shanklin/Ventnor Downs. The land was given by the Warden of Bembridge School and dedicated to the arctic explorer.

1 July 1862

Princess Alice, second daughter of Queen Victoria, married Louis Grand Duke of Hess in the Dining Room at Osborne House. Queen

Victoria, in mourning for her husband, wore black and sobbed throughout the ceremony carried out beneath a portrait of Albert.

7 July 1910
George Clunies Ross, King of the Cocos Islands, died at Ventnor. He was buried at Bonchurch then dug up five years later to be returned to his kingdom.

13 July 1764
Two seamen manhandled a reluctant Henry Fielding ashore at Ryde. His ship had left Tilbury two weeks earlier, being delayed at sea by storms. During that time his wife had suffered a failed attempt to extract aching teeth and Henry had had two litres of liquid withdrawn from his abdomen. The couple stayed at the Nags Head, a mean and squalid pub in Ryde run by the formidable Mrs Francis. After two days, they set sail for Portugal, where Henry died.

17 July 1765
King Charles II landed at Puckaster Cove having endured terrific storms.

18 July 1635
Robert Hooke was born at Freshwater, where his father was curate. When the house in which he was born was pulled down, some of the stone was incorporated in St Agnes Church at Freshwater Bay.

23 July 1865
Queen Victoria's youngest daughter Beatrice, was married at Whippingham Church.

25 July 1626
 St James Church at Yarmouth was consecrated – an annual St James' Day fayre is held on that day.

31 July 1913
John Milne, the 'Father of seismology', died at his home at Shide. He is buried at St Paul's Church, Barton.

10 August 1826
The first recognised race of Cowes Week was held.

14 August 1979
Seventeen sailors died in storms during the 608-mile race from Cowes to the Fastnet Rock off Ireland.

18 August 1934
Four people turned up for the start of a fascist demonstration at Ryde – three of whom were newspaper reporters.

27 August 1979
Lord Louis Mountbatten, the Island's Governor, died in a bomb blast in Ireland.

29 August 1959
A jetty collapsed during the Bembridge Village Diamond Jubilee celebrations, throwing spectators into the sea. The sailing club declared that they had warned of the dangers but the public had been overcome with enthusiasm to witness the greasy pole competition.

8 September 1654
Princess Elizabeth, daughter of Charlies I, died at Carisbrooke Castle three weeks after she and her 8-year-old brother, Henry, had been incarcerated there. On the eve of their father's execution they had been allowed to visit him, when Charles, taking Henry on his knee, had declared, 'they are going to cut off thy father's head.'

9 September 1899
A stone sarcophagus containing a skull was found at Sheepwash Farm, Middleton.

10 September 1866
Ventnor Tunnel opened after two years' gruelling work. It was 1,312 yards long. It closed in 1966 after nearly 100 years' service.

13 September 1647
Robert Hammond, a colonel in the New Model Army, arrived to become the Island's governor. His peaceful refuge was shattered two months later when the king turned up and threw himself on his mercy.

19 September 1908
Cowes councillors were warned that structural damage was caused to property by traction engines speeding through the town.

20 September 1919
Princess Beatrice unveiled Whippingham War Memorial. The first name on the list was her son's, Prince Maurice.

25 September 1998
Newport Fire Brigade were called to their own headquarters when burnt toast set off the fire alarm.

10 October 1908
Mr R Knight of Shanklin was granted a patent for improvements to the rules of croquet.

16 October 1987
Shanklin Pier was blown away in a hurricane.

25 October 1992
The Arch Rock at Freshwater Bay fell into the sea over night.

26 October 1944
Princess Beatrice, the Island's Governor, died.

1 November 1735
John and Charles Wesley arrived at St Helens Bay, moving the next day to Cowes. They seem to have stayed for five weeks, preaching at various locations before leaving for America.

13 November 1647
King Charles arrived on the Isle of Wight, planning to negotiate his way back to the throne.

15 November 1957
The Island's worst air disaster occurred when a flying boat crashed into a disused quarry near Chessel, killing forty-five people.

18 November 1692
The Island's governor, Sir Robert Holmes, died and is buried at Yarmouth.

20 November 1935
John Rushworth, 1st Earl Jellicoe, Governor of New Zealand, died. A memorial plaque was placed in St Boniface Church, where he worshipped when living at St Lawrence Hall.

21 November 1895
Queen Victoria's secretary, Sir Henry Ponsonby, died at Osborne Cottage.

26 November 1959
Albert Ketelby, music hall performer, died at Cowes. He is remembered for renderings of 'In a Monastery Garden' and 'In a Persian Market'.

1 December 1912
Christopher Smith, who named the YMCA, died at Blackgang and was buried at Chale.

5 December 1908
A Cowes labourer was fined for using foul and abusive language to a group of boys who had thrown stones at him as he rode his bicycle. He was told such disgusting language would not be tolerated. (Presumably throwing stones was tolerated.)

14 December 1861
Prince Albert died at Windsor, sending Queen Victoria into a maelstrom of grief. She retreated to Osborne House and refused to leave. On the anniversary of his death seventeen years later, Prince Albert's daughter, Princess Alice, died from diphtheria which she caught from her son.

16 December 1933
Locals attending the Rural District Parish Council meeting complained that having paid the bus fare to get there, the meeting lasted only eighteen minutes. A previous meeting had been terminated after only six minutes.

18 December 1909

Princess Beatrice, patroness of Northwood Choral Society, sang Bizet's grand opera *Carmen* at the Victoria Hall in Cowes (all of it?).

19 December 1889

On the Friday before Christmas, Andrew Templar, a twenty-four-year-old sapper based at Fort Victoria, was delegated to the mess room to hang the decorations. In the process he fell from a ladder and was killed. His funeral took place with full military honours at Yarmouth cemetery, the coffin carried by his comrades from the fort to the graveyard. The Oxford Light Infantry band played the Funeral March, complete with muffled drums. At the graveside, a volley of blank fire ran out across the town.

26 December 1836

Parkhurst children's prison welcomed 102 boys; prior to that they had been housed on a prison hulk moored in the Solent.

Visit our website and discover thousands of other History Press books.

www.thehistorypress.co.uk